By Diane Wakoski

Coins and Coffins (1962)

Four Young Lady Poets (1962)

Discrepancies and Apparitions (1966)

The George Washington Poems (1967)

Inside the Blood Factory (1968)

The Magellanic Clouds (1970)

The Motorcycle Betrayal Poems (1971)

Smudging (1972)

Dancing on the Grave of a Son of a Bitch (1973)

Trilogy: Coin & Coffins, Discrepancies and Apparitions,
    The George Washington Poems (1974)

The Wandering Tattler (1974)

Virtuoso Literature for Two and Four Hands (1975)

Waiting for the King of Spain (1976)

The Man Who Shook Hands (1978)

Trophies (1979)

Cap of Darkness (1980)

The Magician's Feastletters (1982)

The Collected Greed, Parts 1–13 (1984)

The Rings of Saturn (1986)

Emerald Ice: Selected Poems 1962–1987 (1988)

Medea the Sorceress (1991)

Jason the Sailor (1993)

The Emerald City of Las Vegas (1995)

Argonaut Rose (1998)

The Butcher's Apron: New & Selected Poems including
    "Greed: Part 14" (2000)

DIANE WAKOSKI

THE BUTCHER'S APRON

NEW & SELECTED POEMS
INCLUDING "GREED: PART 14"

BLACK SPARROW PRESS · SANTA ROSA · 2000

ACKNOWLEDGMENTS

Thanks to the editors of the following periodicals where some of these poems first appeared: *Black Ox Quarterly, The Country & Abroad, Dead Snake Apotheosis, Many Mountains Moving, Maverick* (an on-line magazine), *Poetry International, Rattle, River City, Seattle Review,* and *Sulfur.*

Black Sparrow Press books are printed on acid-free paper.

LIBRARY OF CONGRESS CATALOGING–IN–PUBLICATION DATA

Wakoski, Diane, 1937–
　　The butcher's apron: new & selected poems including
"Greed: part 14" / Diane Wakoski.
　　　　p.　cm.
　　　ISBN 1-57423-144-8 (paperback)
　　　ISBN 1-57423-145-6 (cloth trade)
　　　ISBN 1-57423-146-4 (signed cloth)
　　　I. Title.
　　PS3573.A42B8　　2000
　　811'.54—dc21　　　　　　　　　　　　　　00-46810

Table of Contents

V. Greed, Part 14: The Greed for Purity

Introduction

MAKING A SELECTED POEMS, if you are as prolific as I have been during the past forty years, is a challenge. *Emerald Ice: Selected Poems 1962-1987* represents what I perceived as my best work when I assembled it in 1987. In the thirteen years since that selection, I have written four new collections of poems, all part of what I call my epic of the West, *The Archaeology of Movies and Books*. I have been thinking of how I could make a new selected poems that would not discount *Emerald Ice* or simply re-collect many of the poems in that volume. I didn't want to rob the most seminal poems from either *Emerald Ice* or the *Archaeologies*, which are on-going and still in print and remain discretely important for reading and understanding my body of work. I also wanted to assemble a book that because it is subject driven might appeal to some readers who are not primarily readers of poetry or who love poetry but haven't previously been introduced to my work.

The fact that made me re-think possibilities for a current selected poems is that I recently completed a new part of my long poem "Greed". This many-parted poem, begun in the late sixties, was collected in 1984 and published as *The Collected Greed: Parts 1-13*. For more than five years it has been out of print. The logical move at this point would have been to reprint *The Collected Greed* and add the new Part 14. However, since so many people already own *The Collected Greed*, it seemed redundant. It also seemed like it might make the new poem invisible, lost in the re-publication of the already known poems. In mulling over these problems, it occurred to me that if I were to assemble a "New and Selected" poems, I could include the new section of "Greed."

This thought led to a longing that had been growing in me for a few years. I had fallen in love with a little pocket anthology that included my poem, "Ode to a Lebanese Crock of Olives" and which was a collection of food poems by many authors. I discovered poems that galvanized me by Kathy Fagan, Colleen McElroy and many other poets both familiar and unfamiliar to me. But most important, it made me realize how many poems I have written over the years concerning food and drink, and the beauty that I have discovered through these subjects.

Enhancing my thoughts along this line was the fact that in all my years of writing and being well published, only once has one of my poems been chosen for the Scribner's annual series *Best Poems of* ———. That poem was "The Butcher's Apron," chosen by Adrienne Rich in 1996, from the magazine *Many Mountains Moving*, a poem describing the acquisition of my aesthetic sensibility via food, and ironically my seeing blood, for the first time, as beautiful food.

All the poems in this collection, including the new "Greed, Part 14," focus on the on-going process of discovering beauty and claiming it for myself. In particular, the still-life presence of food or drink is notably part of this process. For instance, the primal scene that generates the meditations in "Greed, Part 14" is a dinner party, the food of which is described in one of the sections. And one of the dominating tropes of the poem is the chocolate that the little girl, Diane, saves rather than eating. This collection focuses on food, cooking or eating, drinking and, most important, how those images help me define beauty, or the lack thereof.

I noticed when I was compiling the poems that a subsidiary subject is also an important constituent of my aesthetics: flowers. However, I have included in this collection only flower poems, like "Salad Flowers," that actually involve some aspect of food or drink or cooking. I suppose this imagery is connected to my common invocation of the Garden Myth of Judeo-Christian tradition, which of course leads to the dominance of the serpent imagery in the new "Greed, Part 14." I leave that other territory to you, the reader, to explore on your own, since many of those poems filled with flower or plant imagery are contained in either *Emerald Ice* or the four *Archaeologies*.

The easiest way to organize this book would have been chronological, but that seemed to miss the point. I do believe that aesthetics are sometimes landscape derived. This includes the language and idiom which comes out of our individual heritage and culture's landscape. Therefore, I took landscape as my organizing principle.

In the first section, "A California Girl," I concentrate on an important part of my personal mythology: the dominance of images portraying myself as a daughter of the Golden State. In the second section, "The Mirage of Desert and Ocean," I have gathered poems that allude to the polarities of water and the lack of it, a heightened awareness of which anyone growing up in the Southern California that Marc Reisner calls the "Cadillac Desert" must possess. It is almost always through water that landscape becomes a metaphor for me. In the third section, "A California Girl Moves to Michigan Via New York City," I allude to the continental sense I have of myself coming to Michigan where I am spanned to the East and West by oceans. Oddly, moving to New York City and living there during the decade of the sixties emphasized the sense I had of myself being a Westerner, a Californian. In New York I felt the power of my desert landscape more significantly than I ever did when I lived in the West. The Midwest brings a confrontation with dull, plain landscape, in contrast with the magic and brilliance of California and New York.

In the fourth section, "On the Banks of *l'Eau de Vie*," I have tried to indicate moving from the literal landscapes of California, New York City and Michigan to my imaginary world, where I spend time at the Café Eau de Vie. Some of these poems focus on my acceptance of ageing, living in the Midwest, and learning, partly through the aesthetics of food and drink, to live a kind of "still life." The exploration of Diane through her Western beach girl persona, her Medea-life, to her final snaky Medusa self is an important aspect of this book, celebrating the body through food and drink. I have also followed the mysterious path of moon imagery and its connection to water, to explore the meaning of identifying with my name and its antecedent, Diana, the moon goddess.

Some poems that I decided to include may seem like odd choices. For instance, "The Tango Lesson," while about aesthetics, doesn't overtly seem to focus on food or drink; but if you notice the dominating trope—images, words, and references to corn, a food—you will understand my rationale for inclusion. By the same token, there are many poems whose subtext is not simply the comfort provided by a cup of tea, a glass of wine, but actually the aesthetic of beautiful liquids, or the various opacity or transparency of the cup or glass, or the metaphors of sustenance or communion that even a passing reference to food and drink can provide.

The few poems of doom included in this collection—"Whole Sum," "Grain," "What Would Tennessee Williams Have Said,"

"*Orphée*," "Human History: Its Documents" and "The Fear of Fat Children"—are about the disasters of bad food, like sugar, or the inevitable penalties of eating some of the fruit in the Garden.

There is one other anomaly in this collection that I need to point out. I mention this primarily for book collectors who are interested in variorum editions, or readers interested in the way that poems evolve. A small portion of the previously collected poems in this edition have been revised in minor ways. In some cases, my continued thoughts about prosody as it is evinced by line breaks have caused me to alter a whole sequence of delineation in a poem. You will see this most prominently in the poem "Making a *Sacher Torte*." In other cases, a poem which seemed good to me, over the years, began to seem to contain an uncompleted trope or tropes. When I sensed this, I felt compelled to revise the poem slightly. I think of poems such as "*Orphée*" or "Image Is Narrative."

I have cited, with each poem, its source in previous collections, for a number of reasons, one of them being my willingness to make it easy for the reader to compare earlier versions of the poems. This process of revision does not apply to the majority of the poems in this book. However, it is relevant enough that I felt it should be noted. In particular, poems that appeared in magazines but were otherwise previously uncollected have often undergone revision since their first appearance.

As always, I thank my generous and ground-breaking publisher, John Martin, for his long-time support of my work, his sympathy for my aesthetics, and his trust in my poetic meander during our many years of festive association.

I offer also a tribute to the other half of Black Sparrow Press, Barbara Martin, who has for many years now continued to design stylish, elegant and arresting covers for my books. Along with so many of the people these poems name or are dedicated to, Barbara has also provided inspiration via the sophisticated, inventive, and always beautiful food and drink she has prepared and served to me over the years.

Diane Wakoski
February 2000

THE BUTCHER'S APRON

NEW & SELECTED POEMS
INCLUDING "GREED: PART 14"

I | A California Girl

The Butcher's Apron

note: when I was a child, we lived in the midst of
orange groves on Russell Street in East Whittier,
California, just up the road from the Nixon
family grocery store, where I bought my popsicles
from old Mr. and Mrs. Nixon, father and mother
of the late president. When they expanded,
adding a much bigger butcher's counter and a
coffee shop, their son Don Nixon, later featured
in real estate scandals, became the butcher.

for Edward Allen

Red stains on the clean white bib,
the butcher's apron hanging like an abstract expressionist painting,
on the museum wall of my
childhood.

—the most we ever ordered—
a pound of hamburger
to be fried in the black iron skillet
till the edges formed an ugly crust
like a scab on a skinned knee/
The art of the grill
was not found in our manless house.

The beauty of the red on the butcher's
white canvas, which occasionally streaked like an etching
across the white butcher paper
in which he wrapped the chuck, never translated
to the food eaten: grey meats
like steel wool, canned vegetables
with the colors of hospital walls,
sliced white bread like old often-washed
sheets and pillowcases.

My shock one day in the school cafeteria
to see Carol Gregory
    whose mother sewed her
    dresses as elegant as those in
    Vogue magazine
unwrap a waxed paper packet of bright red
meat, in a puddle of something thin and dark/
to realize it was
Roast Beef,
the puddle
was beef blood! There in the Lowell School cafeteria
I saw my first still-life painting, beautiful and
different food among the thermoses
of milk, the wax wrapped peanut
butter or bologna sandwiches. Perhaps
I have added this detail:
    next to Carol's rare roast beef slices,
    another piece of waxed paper on which
    was spread
        several spears of bright green
        asparagus.
Food eaten by kids whose parents were rich
or had been to college
was different,
was like a painting?

My first generation American mother grew up
in a house with a dirt floor, went to school
in a one room schoolhouse. She drank German
coffee instead of milk
as a child. She lifted herself out
of North Dakota, became a bookkeeper
but never learned
about food, the telltale class
marking. In old age, she loves salty things like
Campbell's soups, frozen enchiladas in processed cheese sauce,
bacon white bread sandwiches, and hates the nursing hospital
where they don't salt the food at all.

Plath imagined blood red tulips in white hospitals

as I think of Georgia O'Keeffe's poppies.
My mother who voted for Nixon and hates foreigners
dreams of those red and white cans
which might hold Chicken Noodle or Tomato
soups. She's never heard of Andy Warhol who
mimicked such cans, just as a butcher I talked to in our Michigan
supermarket said that he had never eaten
shrimp, or knew what people did with oxtails. His apron
too had the same bright red stains, not yet faded into
rust. Crimson blood on canvas, the art
of childhood. Unhealed scars,
still capable of bleeding.

from *The Emerald City of Las Vegas*

Breakfast

In the Spanish kingdom
of my living room:
the morning sunshine.
A polished wooden table gleams;
silence is the reflection of burnished woods/pine,
maple, bamboo,
                        waxed to catch the yellow sun.
Outside the wall of windows,
more woods,
these turning to burgundy and gold,
russet,
scarlet,
the wind moving especially
the green leaved ones,
the branches fluttering and bowing,
my courtiers,
my trees.

The kettles boiling now—
            one with water to scald the pot,
            the second with boiling water for the tea.
This morning,
scented Earl Grey,
another courtier, this one perfumed,
a dandy, one of those too-
beautiful men I cannot resist.

On my pine and yellow canvas chair
I rest, drinking the tea,
from a white bone china cup. A remaining crumb
from last night's crusty French bread
is being dazzled on the table's surface/ now
an opal, a pearl, ivory,
a minor jewel dropped from the chest.

In the south window
four sweet basil plants have reached the
height of 18 inches each,
their lime green leaves pungent when
touched/ I give each a little clear water
and pinch off forming bud clusters.

This morning, against all rules,
an egg,
poached in water containing a few drops
of white rice-vinegar, its soft oval body
resting in a poaching cradle of tin,
on three tiny legs, its stiff upright handle
remaining cool
above the boiling white water.

Now, I turn out the egg on a plate
of translucent orange bordered with yellow and black. It
lies there with a vulnerable film over the yolk
while I take my small silver scissors and snip
four large leaves from another basil plant,
this one growing in the kitchen window.
The silver blades slice the leaves in ribbons over
the cooling egg.

Alone, at the kitchen table
with my plate, my single
herbed egg, a goblet of
iced water with a fresh sprig of mint,
also from the kitchen window garden,
and my china cup of hot tea, I sit
down
in my morning kingdom.

Everything
we will ever have
is present
in each day's life. There is no more.
Thus, I need
this morning's royalty,

the immortality of the flesh,
the music of wood,
my perfect view of the autumn swamp.

from *The Magician's Feastletters*
and *Emerald Ice*

The Helm's Bakery Man

The Helm's man came in a yellow truck,
with a hard-shelled top, like a beetle.
Sometimes when I am in bed at night
I remember his donuts and fresh bread,
white-sacked,
sliding out in the smooth wooden tray.

I sleep under a quilt patched with roses and signs of the zodiac.
Nine swords hang over my bed.
In the chest beneath me
are bones.
Each sword has cut some part of me,
and I cling to the sword,
keeping close the memory of an eye or an arm
or a heart.

Sometimes I wake up at night.
Saturn glows like a ruby.
Outside,
around me,
it is dark,
but I hear the flutter of enormous wings.
It is a hard life,
with bones under you
and swords over your head.
But it is everyone's life.
At night under the blanket of the zodiac
I hear a little toot,
see the yellow truck come down my old street;
and there is the Helm's man,
asking what I want today, as I hand him my nickel.
"A bun," I say.

And he gives me one with the moon
in white icing decorating the top.

from *Discrepancies & Apparitions*
and *Emerald Ice*

Saturday Night

for Barbara Drake

The muddy tangled week
was over
and Saturdays would be
late breakfast, a trip in the rattletrap Chevy to town
the weekly luxury of library,
department store,
shop windows,
and then supper out
and a movie.

We always had our supper at a sandwich shop
with polished Formica counter and tables,
the soda machines gleaming stainless,
the shiny nozzles on the ice cream counter spotlessly
holding their chocolate, cherry, vanilla, coke
syrups.
We were usually there about 5 p.m.
when he had only a few customers, as he
closed at 6
on Saturdays.
Each week my mother would suggest I order something
different.
But I was firm,
what I wanted
never varied.
A ham sandwich on toasted white bread with
mayonnaise served with potato chips and one slice of pickle
and a small coke. While my sister and
adventurous mother
would
each week
try little hamburgers,

bacon and tomato sandwiches
egg salad
grilled cheese,
culinary explorers, never repeating as
I,
unwaveringly,
ate my ham
sandwich,
drank my coke. After all,
for a child who drank a quart of milk a day,
scorned common (Wonder) bread,
ate almost no sugar and whose
diet seldom contained any meat
but ground beef,
this seemed like
the most exotic meal in the world.

My favorite theater was The Whittier
on Whittier Blvd. It
had holes in the ceiling
which simulated stars.
The heavens twinkled as you watched
Betty Grable,
Gene Kelly,
Fred Astaire,
June Allyson,
my mother's favorites: Technicolor musicals.

What a feeling,
coming home in the darkness, Saturday nights,
having spent the day in town,
eaten my ham sandwich,
gone to the library,
gone window-shopping
and seen the movie. Tucked on the floor of the car
beneath my feet
were my six library books, the limit allowed to each
person. Wealth,
rubies and diamonds, my week of reading,
though I would probably finish them all

by Monday.

I often fell asleep in the old car
as it traveled out of town
into the orange groves where we lived.
When we arrived
and my mother woke me up,
I would fuss to stay in the car all night.
I still think each morning
when I wake up and don't want to face the day
of how I felt then, not wanting to emerge
from the dusty old car,
wanting to snuggle down into the warm
backseat while it carried me through the night
of fragrant oranges.
a treasure of books at my feet
in a world where I could always be the princess,
never the servant,
never the poor peasant, living alone
in the country
with only an old mother.

from *The Magician's Feastletters*

The Lessons of Smoked Fish, Bear Claws
& American Barbecue

thinking of Colleen McElroy's poem
"To Market, to Market"

Robert's new grill is on the motor rotisserie,
the juices of a chicken seeping, gathering, then plummeting
to the silver foil catch pan over the coals. Every Saturday morning
there is someone out there with a power mower, even in this little
neighborhood
with diploma-sized lawns, lots of student tenants
and a fairly small variety of
birds.

I too learned the sound of the Ice Cream Truck
tinkling through East Whittier or La Habra
roller-skating-bike-riding-lots-of-library-books school vacations,
and I also had different urges.
It was the toot of the little horn on the bakery truck,
not the ice cream wagon,
that lured me from wherever I was,
reading or playing with paper dolls.
My own salivary juices sloshed
around when my ear caught the wooden click
of the drawers in the Helm's Bakery Truck, the wax paper
serviettes that the baker's driver crinkled and whispered
over the warm icing. My nose drawn
to the risen yeast, the scent of
Bear Claws and Raisin Cinnamon Buns. Sugar
was never so inviting.

I wish, like Colleen who grew up in St. Louis, that I had had the
     essential
wisdom of taste to go for smoked fish,

sashimi moments,
salty roe on a cracker.
After all, I was a sailor's
daughter. But I graduated low, or average,
in the class of food tastes.
My nickel bought an Abba Zaba, peanut butter taffy bar
that was long and had
more chewing time. I
admit to it. There was once a time when
sugar bewitched me, even though I wanted to be
different.

Late summer and these birds are eating our seeds;
now the Nuthatch lands for a sleek black-headed bite,
moves back to the trunk
of the Locust where he walks upside-down.
Red Cardinal is like the red Kool-Aid which healed
our hot throats, bad for us
with red dye numbered poison.
I don't know if the female Cardinal
who only blushes red from her brown coat
is anything like me. She takes her presence for granted,

whereas I feel left out
on this Saturday morning, defined
by men mowing,
grilling,
taking care of
the orderly world I love
and the birds that inhabit its backyard.
My only contribution is the Moonflower,
one of which is trumpeting white,
as big as a street lamp
on its desert stalk this morning.
American Saturday morning.
Red Cardinal,
Old Blue Jay,
White Moon Flower.

"Stop flashing,"

I tell the birds. "Stop flashing," I say.
Your beauty is beyond what I can order. In fact,
I am not the Orderer in my life. I am the Observer
of beauty, of Saturday morning order. I only
see where it is and where it is not. I
know the falseness of sugar
but was never wise enough, like Colleen, to prefer smoked fish.
I am full of failed memories. Locked in
the Midwest, away from the salty ocean and
the smoky odors of old boats,
away from the essential sex
of this universe

which cannot be sugar.

When Canned Peaches Turn into Maplelight

It glows
the small yellow maple
behind the picket fence in grey
autumn damp.
It's like a bowl of commercially canned
peaches, smooth, shiny globes from being skinned,
cut by machine, loaded with
sugar syrup which makes them shine
like greasepaint under klieg lights.

For years they've both been there,
the tree and the image:
one moment which has no meaning to me
except as an emblem of pain, defeat,
impossible failure.
Sitting at the metal kitchen
dinette table in Southern California of the fifties,
blue cardiganned elbows
resting on metal, the bowl with the one
glistening peach half in its clear syrup in front of me,
a dimestore spoon, blue and white kitchen
curtains, late afternoon in California's
linoleum autumn, feeling sorry for myself,
knowing I was trapped, a pregnant girl
with no husband, one who knew how lonely
a child is without a father, one who knew how
terrible the poverty of white-collar working mothers could be,
one who hated women with no life but children and earning a
    living,
one who wanted to define herself differently
and now was trapped, eating an unhealthy, unattractive
commercially canned peach, an image of her mother's life
where you played bad music by ear and only watched Hollywood
musicals because the good movies were about problems

and who wanted to watch other people suffering?

Like several hundred garish, unreal-looking
canned peach halves, the leaves on my Michigan
backyard maple wave at me.
They have turned into a beauty
I never expected, one I longed for but never
hoped I would actually achieve.
How can I reject old age, then,
or death if it is all part of this transformation?
I am still the girl sitting at the white metal table
crying into sugar, eating sunshine
in whatever form I can get it.

from *Jason the Sailor*

Un Morceau en Forme de Poire

for Thomas Parkinson

Sitting on my kitchen
butcher block table,
in its yellow enameled cast iron pot,
is the remains of a liquid for poaching pears
which contains caterpillars of lemon peel
and centipede lengths of vanilla bean.
The morning kitchen has a country smell,
for my sink is stopped up
and I couldn't wash the dishes last night
after working on my Hazelnut Chocolate Pear Torte,
and the thick porcelain jacketed top of my *bain-marie* has smudges
like muddy prints
over its lips, waiting for sudsy hot water and a drain
that will work.

The fragrance of vanilla and chocolate and pear mingle
with some beets and onions, waiting on the counter
for soup.
Reminding me of a moment
in my life
which perhaps was a bridge between
the girl who ate ham sandwiches on white
bread with mayonnaise & a pickle
on Saturday evenings,
as an after-library-and-shopping treat,
and the woman who now makes *Sacher Tortes*,
linguine al pesto,
or stuffed vine leaves
commonly on Saturday nights.

This scene from the '50s:
        wearing the cap of darkness,

I go to babysit for some young university faculty.
Entering their house in the Berkeley hills, I see
plain pine floors with
threadbare Oriental carpets,
bookshelves made of boards and bricks,
hand thrown pottery.
They leave, and I hold the baby
as he cries himself to sleep.
Then I wander about the small house into the kitchen
where every dish, glass, pot or pan
seems to be dirty on the sink,
the kitchen table holding Chemex coffee pot with a bit of
amber liquid
in the bottom,
next to it, on a saucer, a paper filter full of wet grounds.
The whole kitchen was permeated
with the smell of vanilla biscuits,
and a mingle of other interesting possibilities. Some
leeks? The Viennese Roast coffee beans? Some rusks
which were also lying out?
For the first time in my life
I witnessed a soiled kitchen, used by sloppy people,
which seemed wholesome, the dirt and insects of gardens, rather
        than
neglect;
fragrant
with good food and even
a good life. Of course I spent
the evening washing the dishes,
and cleaning the kitchen,
embarrassing the good-livers when they came home,
who felt required to offer me
more money.
                What a difference
between my mother's sense of good food
(baked ham and canned peas)
and this kitchen,
redolent with rosemary, lamb shoulder and garlic,
an odor I didn't know then, because I thought garlic was a stale-
white powder with a slightly bitter taste.

34

That moment
going into the kitchen
gave me a new possibility for ORDER.
Am I destined,
I wonder,
to go back to the Berkeley hills someday
and live in such a house,
the messy interesting life of those young intellectuals? My own
kitchen here in the midwest has acquired
some of its jumble.

Perhaps last night
across the continent
that couple, now undoubtedly in their 60s
woke up
to a distant fragrance
of poaching pears,
a torte baking,
the ganache cream being stirred with its 15 ounces of chocolate?

Perhaps, in a dream, they saw me
as an old woman of the earth,
holding their son by the heel,
immersing him in the fire of my passionate need
trying to forge the armor of immortality
as he cried himself to sleep,
after which I went into the kitchen
and ritually cleansed it,
leaving some clarity, leaving it renewed,
and taking with me the knowledge
of common chaos,
mortal beauty,
smelling of vanilla,
an earthy bean.

from *The Magician's Feastletters*
and *Emerald Ice*

Amaryllis on Thames

I called Alice, but she was
cooking pasta. I tried to find her lettuces
but they were so small I could not even compare them
to the gold stars on my good piano lesson page,
and one day when the thick crust of a baguette
tripped me, I bled coffee. Only one
town this could be, and it isn't LA!

Night Blooming Jasmine

It wasn't on Crete, but in the hills of Berkeley
where the Daughter disappeared. And forget crocus. It
was the pink rhododendrons, like festival lanterns
or sunsets over the bay, which attracted her.
Their season is the season of that town.
The Maybeck houses
with their brown woody, thrush-y sides
grow like hedgehog mushrooms, out of the slopes.
She lives there, hidden all winter in one of them,
and then like Garbo going out for groceries
in her shades, spring
      with tulip trees and Hawthorn,
      with azalea, the pinks and whites, not even her colors,
      not the girl in the swing ruffled with the beauty
      men do not know how
      to touch—spring
brings her out, could that be?

No, she is going for *The New York Times*, she is slim
in her dark clothes, she has cheek bones and ankles
that the screen will notice. She is not made to protest
war or the loss of free speech, she is made for a dark espresso
bar, a grocery
smelling of fresh pasta and tins of tomato paste,
the coffee bean store with vials and philters, and alchemical
ways of extracting aromas,
her foot in its thin shoe, entering the bakery,
the boulangerie, where long sticks of bread or round pannikins
of whole grain are waiting.
This is the town where poets lurk, and books contain
musical notes often stamped with gold leaf. It is the
place where you learn that everything has a skeleton, a structure
of bones which is more important than the flesh, so
changeable, that covers them.

Corn bread here is
a sculpture of meal and moisture. Polenta a cake
stirred until the spoon stands alone in the mixture, where
soft things gain stiffness, it is the place where wine can be truly
conceived of, if not made, and it is where everyone learns to be
an architect.

I envy those who dwell in this city, the
bones of the world, I call them. Am a different
kind of Daughter than the Mistress of Chez Panisse,
or the woman who taught me I could not be a pianist.
Not elegant-boned, more a carapace,
I walk through the streets, wearing my own shades, disguised
as one of the young, oh so sad, bums, an alcoholic cloud
of Night Blooming Jasmine wafting from my moonlit hair.
You'd never know it was the city of rebirth—
a concept incomplete without a sojourn underground
coming first. I know what happens when you look back/
I'm not doing that. Some part of me never left;

I belong to the place
        like the Maybeck houses,
                the Edward Teller of the Atomic Bomb,
                        and in the fragrance of night blooming jasmine
                the Greta Garbo women cooking
                alone.

from *Argonaut Rose*

In San Francisco

there is no hunger, though many
eat only poor man's bread:
pine cones and coffee.

Making a Sacher Torte

Her hands, like albino frogs,
on the keys of a Bosendorfer,
nails short and thin like sliced almonds, fleshy fingers,
with the lightning bolt gold and diamond wedding
ring, zigzagging up to her fat knuckle,
looking out of place
on the heavy working hand.

Forty-five and fashionable,
with knit suits and suede pumps on thin-ankled feet,
short, curly blond hair and her big Jewish nose,
her husband a jeweler and she, with her rich German accent,
my piano tutor.

I, 19, and wearing home-made cotton dresses with gathered skirts,
the Niagara Falls in my eyes, no wedding, no wedding,
a girl with nothing but soapy hands and wet heart, a big
    frog-like brain;
I loved her for listening to me.
On the black piano bench, I was still the little princess whose
    golden
ball had rolled into a well, and she,
the Frog Prince, lifted it out
with webbed hands, tossing it in the light, the gold
of her lightning bolt wedding ring catching the sun, as she gave
    me
her gold, the talk, the princess world of pianos, converting me
from Chopin who had a perfect hand, like a water lily,
to Beethoven's last work, fashioned with shovels and clubs
and the Germanic ear for long phrases, never-ending sentences
    who
too must have had hands that looked more like
pads than the lily.

Near Christmas, she asked me one afternoon,
"Do you know what I have spent the last two days doing
with these hands?"
            (spreading them out,
            heavy and short-nailed against the piano keys)
"Grinding nuts in a mortar. For a torte."

And she continued to talk
about her culinary activities which then
seemed exotic then to me
and which I only recalled today after I had whirled
some almonds in my Cuisinart and was folding
them into meringue for a *Sacher Torte*.
Living a life so remote from those sad Berkeley days
when I was a poor student, poor adolescent, girl from the working
            classes,
where the piano bench, hard seat, was the only one I wanted,
on which I sat for hours most days,
beating my hands on the keys, out of love,
as she had ground those nuts
by hand for her family's holiday cake.

We often talked of our favorite books and both of us
were then avidly reading Salinger's stories as they were
published in *The New Yorker*.
I, wishing the Glass family were my own
and she, preaching, of all
things,
about how I should have more charitable feelings for my mother.

Yet, my own mother had none of the attributes
which made Mrs. Ury
so compelling to me; for it was not just
those hours at the piano
that made me cherish her. She was a bold and intelligent
woman who had forced her family to understand the danger
in Germany and arranged
for them to leave before the disaster
of the camps. She lived in a
world of books and pianos,

had gone on tour all over the world,
could make her Linzer Torte without any machine.
She spoke two
languages flawlessly and was generous of spirit,
though a perfection-
ist of craft,
to this provincial girl
who couldn't play the piano very
well.

She talked to me by the hour,
wearing elegant clothes, and
praised me when I deserved it. Once,
I remember her telling me about
practicing the piano in winter in Germany, when
she was a student,
wearing wool gloves with the finger-ends
cut off, because it was
so cold in the studio. She gave
me a sense of the meaning of sacri-
fice, and in retrospect
what I feel my own family
most deprived me of was
that meaning.
          That if you practiced the piano in a studio at 45
          degrees in winter
          it was in order to become an exceptional performer
          of the world's great piano music.

          That those same hands
          wearing a $10,000 ring
          30 years later,
          could perform the same kind of act,
          as a ritual for her family,
          grinding the nuts for the Christmas torte,
          when, of course, her maid could
          have done it
          just as well.

And me for, a new meaning for the Frog Prince:

Not the lover,
whose kindness made him beautiful.
That seems like a small meaning for the fairy tale.
Rather, that the
transformation itself
of Frog into Prince can happen.
      That Mrs. Ury,
      with her great frog hands, who could play with the
      verve of Rubinstein
      and the delicacy of Gieseking,
      rescued the ball of gold
      after it rolled into the well,
      gave me her German self as mother,
      gave me a new history,
      gave me her heritage,
for though I have not
become a concert pianist,
I have accepted the tradition of the keyboard artists.
And her great gift to me:
to show me that impossible as it was
for me to be a musician
in fact
this did not deprive me of music,
but gave it back to me in more complex ways.
As the torte was baking in the oven today,
I wondered idly about
how different my life would have been
had Tanya Ury actually been my mother. But
of course the truth is
that she was;
how accidental is blood; how meaningless
the connection of birth.

I look in the pond,
a mirror full of lilies whose long root systems curl up from the
chocolatey mud and whose green leaves
might hold one of those
green music makers. In it
I see nothing but the reflection of sunlight, a golden spot
which must be projected through the thick lenses of my glasses.

As I move my face, the golden
spot dances and rolls over the water,
over the lily pads, occasionally
reflecting and glittering off one of the pale pink flower buds;
experience and memory are my real roots,
tangled, complicated, all the freeways
I have traveled to
reach this moment when I lift the firm almond torte
out of the oven.

from *The Magician's Feastletters*
and *Emerald Ice*

Peaches

Soft baskets full of their yielding flesh
ripening at once
overwhelmingly
the sugar bleeding from spots where the skin
slides away.
This mid-summer luxuriance
falling somewhere
in muffled thuds from the trees,
the small scimitar-shaped leaves cling to a few stems
like green mustaches.

Somewhere in California
my blood line goes on,
making me unnecessary.
I'm just another soft peach
which should quickly be preserved
or eaten
in the cool morning,
the sanguine juice
making each finger
momentarily fragrant.

　　My silence means
nothing
or so many things
one cannot take it
　　　　　　　　personally.

from *The Magician's Feastletters*

Ode to a Lebanese Crock of Olives

for Walter's Aunt Libby's
diligence in making olives

As some women love jewels
and drape themselves with ropes of pearls, and stud their ears
with diamonds, band themselves with heavy gold,
have emeralds on their fingers or
opals on white bosoms,
I love the still life
of grapes whose skins frost over with the sugar forming inside,
hard apples, and delicate pears;
cheeses,
from the sharp fontina, to icy bleu,
the aromatic *chèvres, boursault, boursin,* a litany of
thick breads, dark wines,
pasta with garlic,
soups full of potato and onion;
and butter and cream,
like the skins of beautiful women, are on my sideboard.

These words are to say thank you
to
Walter's Aunt Libby
for her wonderful olives;
oily green knobs in lemon
that I add to the feast when they get here from Lebanon
where men are fighting, as her sisters have been fighting
for years, over whose house the company stays in
and whose recipes for kibbee or dolmas or houmas
are passed along.

I often wonder,
had I been born beautiful,
a Venus on the California seashore,

46

if I'd have learned to eat and drink so well?
For, with hummingbirds outside my kitchen window
to remind of small elegance,
and mourning doves in the pines & cedar, speaking with grace,
and the beautiful bodies
of lean blond surfers,
dancing on terraces,
surely had I a beautiful face or elegant body,
surely I would not have found such pleasure
in food?
I often wonder why a poem to me
is so much more like a piece of bread and butter
than like a sapphire?
But with mockers flying in and out of orange groves,
and brown pelicans dipping into the Pacific,
looking at camellias and fuchsia,
an abundance of rose, and the brilliant purple ice plant
which lined the cliffs to the beach,
life was a "Still Life" for me.
And a feast.
I wish I'd known then
the paintings of Rubens or David,
where beauty was not only
thin, tan, California girls,
but included all abundance.

As some women love jewels,
I love the jewels of life.
And were you,
the man I love
to cover me (naked) with diamonds,
I would accept them too.

Beauty is everywhere,
in contrasts and unities.
But to you, I could not offer the thin tan fashionable body
of a California beach girl.
Instead, I could give the richness of burgundy,
dark brown gravies,
gleaming onions,

the gold of lemons,
and some of Walter's Aunt Libby's wonderful olives from Lebanon.

Thank you, Aunt Libby,
from a failed beach girl,
out of the West.

from *Waiting for the King of Spain*
and *Emerald Ice*

My Mother's Milkman

Cloyce Hamilton,
a slender tan man in white uniform,
with gold teeth,
the truck stopping with foot-clack suddenness
on the gravel road,
the carrier holding four glass bottles of whole milk
with their little paper caps crimped over
the tops.

My mother in her navy blue wool bathrobe
standing by the blue and white tile
kitchen sink, drinking her first morning cup of coffee.

She opens the door for Cloyce
and they stand talking,

for eight years,
three days a week, the Pellissier Dairy Truck
stops with its standing milkman-driver,
Cloyce Hamilton, dressed in white, his suntanned long
wrists and hands emerging from
white starched sleeves,
my mother's King of Spain.

Sometimes my mother ironing in the kitchen
or just drinking her coffee.
Waiting to exchange a few words, or
to catch a glimpse of Cloyce Hamilton or
sometimes
to give him a cup of coffee and listen
to the story of his life.
She loved to hear
how a man suffered and longed beyond his milkman's life.

My mother and sister and I
visited the Hamiltons sometimes.
Their house was carpeted, dark, and had
a gold-framed oil painting of a California desert scene
over the mantel.
Vera wore her dark hair in a bun, was handsome,
their house smelled like mothballs and I
envied them; they were typical,
the average American family.
Handsome father who drove his milk truck every day.
Handsome mother who had her dining room table
polished and a gold-
framed oil over the mantel.
Two plump girls who wore (and how I envied them)
patent leather shoes.

In my early adolescence
I remembered long murmured conversations between my mother
and Cloyce Hamilton, and then one day
she said we were going to visit Cloyce, that he was no
longer living with Vera and the girls.
We went to a tiny house by the
railroad tracks. Inside was the handsome Cloyce and a big teen-
aged boy. I don't remember the boy's name. But
Cloyce wanted to adopt the boy, said my mother, and bring
him home, and I gathered the whispered conversations had been
about his struggle with Vera.

How my mother loved to sympathize with men
about their struggles with their wives.
My poor, sad, husbandless mother. The closest
she ever came to seduction—
listening to the whispers of angry
or frustrated men
about their own sad, faithful wives.
Cloyce finally left wife and daughters to live
with this tough, homeless boy.

None of it quite made sense to me. I questioned and questioned
    my mother who was a

scorpion-like listener, with her secrets,
dark pools in which undetermined creatures swam.
Now, in retrospect, the story of my mother's milkman
still seems veiled. And sad.
She, such a lonely woman, getting up
each morning for her handsome milkman
who lived the family life she yearned for, and he,
tortured, wanting only the
love of a young
boy.

What I remember often is this scene:
 the Hamilton's dark house,
 the gold-framed painting of the Sonoran desert
 glowing in the room across from the polished dining room
 table,
 the smell of mothballs,
 the dark Vera, like a Spanish lady,
 and the smell of darkness itself
 in the house.

My mother, believing to the end
that Cloyce only wanted a son,
never admitting her handsome milkman,
King of Spain,
loved boys.

After all those years of waiting
in the kitchen, at dawn, for the thick milk which she put
in her German coffee.

Drinking.
Fourteen cups a day.
Relieving the black caffeine bitterness
with cream from California's
Pellissier Dairy.

from *Cap of Darkness*

Love to My Electric Handmixer

with apologies to André Breton

My electric handmixer of 87 bloodstone finches,
my electric handmixer of a house on fire,
my electric handmixer of sunflower petals,
my electric handmixer of clenched teeth,
my electric handmixer of gold in the sea water,
my electric handmixer of carboned tunnels,
my electric handmixer of frequent metallic rain,
my electric handmixer of sugar beet oceans,
my electric handmixer of lemon ears,
I am happier with you than
lifting leather cushions and finding spongy gold.
I am happier with you than
electing a cowboy to office.
I am happier with you than
the United State Navy.
O, electric handmixer, I would put your
names on the wings of gypsy moths,
for love.

from *The Magellanic Clouds*

Perfume

It started with my mother's Shalimar. So
few images of richness
in our two-room shack in the orange groves
during WW II. But my Navy daddy, with his white sailor
hat and wool big collared middies
would come home with presents, bargain luxuries
either from the PX or
foreign travel without duty: satin heart-
shaped boxes of candy,
beaten silver cups from India
and always for my mother,
the French perfume, a crystal bottle
shaped like a scallop, named
for an exotic garden misspelled,
Shalimar

How a little girl saw a woman: wrapped in perfume.
Fifty dollars a bottle in 1942. Two week's salary for
my mother, the bookkeeper.
She saved it for special occasions.

My mother most of the time had the
aroma of a cheap bath powder, Cashmere Bouquet, or dimestore
perfume, and my father of Old Spice after shave.
I didn't like those smells,
the former reminding me of a body like
a raw oyster that
no one could want to touch;
the latter of my happy daddy who brought presents
and then departed, leaving us poor
and in misery, three females in a dusty
house with bare yard and broken

53

screens.

What, then, were the
fragrances of childhood
that lured me?
    The stationery store with its
    crisp boxes of Crane's laid bond, parchment, or faux vellum
        papers,
    the smell of formal invitations, and Parker pens,
    the expensive kind my mother owned to ply her
        bookkeeper's trade,
    writing tiny, neat figures into thick ruled ledgers.
    The smell of money,
    of wealth,
    expensive paper and fine nibbed pens.

    And starch, the hot iron gliding over starched
cotton blouses and dresses, my mother taking in ironing
to add to her meager bookkeeper's income. I would wake up
in summer, to morning doves chortling
outside, and the smell
    of hot slick cloth,
my mother standing at the ironing board,
the beautiful causeway of smooth shirts, ruffled
curtains, steaming their starched patina
into the breakfast air,
    fresh bookish morning, a little like library paste,
always an aroma children find enticing. I would
stretch in my top bunk bed,
listen to the doves, ruffling their throats
outside, feel
the radiance of morning itself
and the comfort, the security of the warm
ironed clothes
and household items,
gathering on hangers at the door.
    The smell of cleanliness and order.

Then the fat lady with her shopping bags,
who walked up from Santa Fe Springs Road to

54

take care of us
when Mama went to work.
    She gusted a smell of Juicy Fruit gum,
    and cherry life savers.
Her multi–layered bags,
old and worn as Chinese museum silks,
were full of sweet things,
candies and
cookies, her snacks for
the day, all wrapped in the perfect silver
swirl of Juicy Fruit gum,
    a smell like ripe bananas.

And the yardage store. When I got old
enough to use the treadle sewing machine
and even before I began to sew
it beckoned.
    There among the bolts of cotton goods especially
I imagined living in a mansion, with velvet drapes made from
cylinders and rolls of fabric, with crisply tailored sofas covered
with chintz, wound on long tubes and so much
wider than the other cloths, so stiff
it would stand up alone.

Each case of spooled silk and cotton thread,
gleaming as if it were bird plumage, was like
a jewelry box; and I lingered over embroidery floss
whose colors glowed in slinky Technicolor.
Walking the aisles of fabric,
I imagined myself wearing taffeta evening gowns
with giant bows, Edith Head costumes,
perky Doris Day peau de soie swirling skirted dresses,
or slim satin cocktail gowns, all sewn from
these intact and complete cloths, these delicate as
Audrey Hepburn dimities flocked with blue cornflowers,
and the cards of lace that might trim the tissue cotton
into a fluffy blouse, or a night gown.
    The smell of female beauty, lined up
    as perfectly articulated
    bolts of fabric.

Teenage life brought me a hand lotion
that was beautiful to my eyes, as the ocean. It was a
pale aquamarine color, the color of the fifties.
     And its fragrance was the coolness that I hoped
     to acquire, the smooth perfect girl I wanted to be,
     everything starched into stillness, each page
     of writing paper blank and waiting for
     insignias of black ink.
I wrote on grey paper,
an affectation, and wore Aquamarine Lotion, the
     tile and ice fragrance of a non-briny sea.
     How carefully I laid myself out,
     to smell of perfection,
     coolness,
     starched order,
     apart from the raw world.

I think of Berkeley as smelling
     like coffee, also a fragrance I loved from
my childhood, not knowing then that the perfection of coffee
was a fresh ground bean. Its fragrance
     wrapped round me, as I sat
     in cafes, wrote harlequin poems,
     and no longer smelled like Aquamarine.

New York City was the scent of books and curry.
Vital organic smells, that had nothing to do with anyone's body
though they were such physical odors.
Such an old city, and old buildings, filled
with bookstores where silverfish scurried out of
each volume as you opened it, and mildew
     was also a smell of learning and reading. Coffee houses
          often
     smelled like cinnamon, and delis smelled of pickles
     and herring.
I began to think about wearing perfume.
A woman wore
expensive perfume, and if a man
didn't bring it as a present,
she bought it for herself. It was her sign.

The prices steep always,
and now we are in an era of spray bottles, and
thus larger volume. Now, it's not perfume but
eau de toilette or *eau*
de cologne. The concentrated essence, the perfume itself
too heavy, too hard to use.
We moved from the age of musk
to the age of airy scent, away from the glass
stopper rubbed against
the wrist and at the ear pulse,
to the cloud of droplets
vaporized around our bodies,
the spray of scent
     like petals all over our bodies.

I found a perfume finally.
Like my mother's,
it was a Guerlain, French and
pricey fragrance,
    "Mitsouko"
      so delicate you almost can't smell
      it on my body, light and dark
      at the same time.
I love to open my closet
and smell it hovering lightly over the rack
emanating from the sleeves
and lapels. So many years now
of Mitsouko. Occasionally exchanged for other
crushes, "Diorissimo," "Ysatis," but always
I return to the subtle one,
"Mitsouko,"
that disappears everywhere except
in my closet

PART II. BELLE DU JOUR

Last month, while listening to an NPR interview with Catherine Deneuve, I heard a usually sensitive and smart interviewer ask a question that shocked me. Not just for its ageism, but for its assumptions about aesthetics, I think. Terry Gross of "Fresh Air," usually such a good interviewer, talked generally with Deneuve, then introduced a bit of chat about her work with Richard Avedon in making Shalimar commercials, interesting in itself as Deneuve talked about how she really enjoyed being photographed for ads, how she entered into the enterprise as seriously as a film and did not consider it simply hack work to make money,

What Terry Gross asked Catherine Deneuve was, "Do you *still* wear perfume?" I am to this minute completely stunned by this, wondering where such a question came from! Why would a woman, just because she is aging stop wearing perfume?

Catherine Deneuve has been generally described as one of the most beautiful actresses in the world. I concur with this description entirely. Even in her latest films, where she is in her sixties, she is more beautiful than most women ever dream of being at sixteen or twenty-one. Yet, Terry Gross's question seemed to strip her of this.

I suppose, since I am also someone who loves perfume and regards it as more than an enhancement of life like good food, interesting wine or books, I think of it as something a person wears all the time, whether alone or in company, to bed alone or with a lover, even when she is working. I wear perfume in the same way I use soap or deodorant, and don't plan to stop using any of those items just because I get old. I know that some people don't care for perfumes, as they don't drink wine or go to the opera. Perhaps they think of perfume the way I think of diamonds or cosmetics, simply not to their taste. But if I loved them, I cannot imagine giving up any of those things because of age. Of course one's taste or style might change somewhat, thinking what would seem best on an older body. But why would you want your body to smell less good because you are old? The idea that someone could love perfume when they are young and then want to give up wearing it after they reach sixty or seventy, or even eighty or ninety simply because they are old, seems absurd to me.

Perhaps over the years one might change one's perfume, as the varieties are endless. And if Deneuve had said that when she was making the commercials she wore a certain Guerlain perfume, but now as she grows older she prefers a different kind of fragrance, this might have made sense of a question like "do you *still* wear perfume?" (I.e. "do you *still* wear the same perfume?") But what transpired in this interview seemed to contain an assumption on Terry Gross's part that women only wear perfume when they are young and seductive. Then a cutoff point, say age sixty, comes and they stop wearing perfume. She seemed to imply that there would probably be no point, even if you were Catherine Deneuve, the most beautiful woman in the world, to wear perfume when you were older and of course therefore not seductive.

In fact, the question contained so many negative assumptions, or perhaps naive ones (has Terry Gross herself never worn perfume except on a special date; does she have just one $90 bottle of perfume that she can't even use up in ten years because she only puts it on once a month?), that I almost started jumping around waving my arms as I heard it. Deneuve, always cool and sophisticated, simply replied, "Of course I wear it, even now that I live in the country."

Thus, this elegant and always gracious woman dignified Terry Gross's insulting question to the extent of implying that one could understand that Gross might perceive perfume as an Apollonian city artifact, not appropriate to rustic or agrarian life.

In fact, the more I meditate on this, the more it seems as if Terry Gross had a kind of 19th century naiveté, as well as an ageist vision of the world. Her attitude: not only would it be improper or at least exotic for a plain or country girl to wear perfume, it would be totally without propriety for an older woman to wear it? In fact, Terry Gross's question "Do you still wear perfume?" made her sound as if she, Terry Gross, were about twelve years old and couldn't even conceive what it was like to be thirty, to say nothing of fifty, sixty, seventy, etc.

I've always been impressed with this reporter who, while she has a genuineness about her and occasionally suggests a modest opinion, also has an enthusiasm that is nice in an interviewer and never argues with her guests, even when they probably are offending her, and usually always stands back and lets them talk after she introduces pithy questions. I have never heard her ask a really insensitive question before.

Still smarting from my irritation at Terry Gross that night, I watched a charming film from 1997 on video, *I Love You, I Love You Not*, which features the aging and now quite fat (!) Jeanne Moreau of *Jules and Jim* (Truffaut) fame. I was impressed with the willingness of a beautiful actress who no longer is beautiful (unlike Deneuve) to appear unselfconsciously on screen wearing tent-like dresses, still flaunting shoulder-length blonde (a wig? dyed?) hair, and having fun with an almost adolescent exuberance, interacting with the character played by the young Claire Danes. It seemed clear to me that Moreau was wearing fashions appropriate to the nineties with no concern about her own aging body, and that she enjoyed her long hair regardless of ageist propriety, and undoubtedly was (Oh, how shocking, Terry) wearing perfume.

It is very hard, aging. And it must be multiplied when you've been famous as one of the most beautiful actresses in the world. I don't think we really understand very much about getting older, and the fact that in many ways we do change as we age seems to obscure the reality that we probably don't change in the ways that old age changes are stereotyped. A beautiful woman is almost always beautiful until she dies, barring disfiguring illness, and a woman who has loved perfume all her life, having once become an icon of *Vogue* magazine and other perfume commercials, is not going to stop wearing it.

I didn't come away from the interview with Deneuve, one of my favorite actresses (*Belle du Jour* is my movie), thinking and knowing more about her, as I should have. Instead, I came away wondering what is wrong with Terry Gross? Alas, the answer is that she is simply reflecting common American ideas about age and sophistication. Very negative ideas. And probably very stereotyped. Alas, alas. In some respects, we remain *the truly* "Ugly Americans" Europeans described in the fifties of this century.

Part III. Autumn

Robert is tearing up the summer garden
and today, he's brought into
the dining room great bunches
of herbs. Tied up with green hemp cord,
the tall-as-a-Chinese-fan bunch of sage
has a silver sheen and emits an odor of pungent
suggestions. For instance, a roasting chicken stuffed with onions,
dry bread and sage.

The bunch of thyme is springy
like a head of newly washed hair, or green feathers you might
stuff into a doll's pillow. It wafts the delicate scent
of a path trodden on by two lovers,
or the smell of a child's clean hand.

The slightly gawky lengths of tarragon wave at me
with their licorice fragrance and invite me to
combine them, not as herbs but as cut flowers, with some red
        salvia
of little odor at all, just a decorative annual still growing
in the garden where Robert hasn't yet tilled.
I put this bouquet on a shelf above my crimson movie-watching
        chair
to flutter down on me the scent of a light cream sauce
for a salmon
or the sweet bite of it in' rice vinegar
to dress some greens.

For weeks now
I've been cutting the long branches of sweet
basil into huge swards
and thrusting them into tall pitchers. Now most of the basil
is in full bloom,
its white little orchid flowers, multitudes lining
each frond, are almost
as fluffy as cherry blossoms in the spring.
The odor of the basil
is earthy, even rank at certain moments

of the day, then a fallen
leaf might get crushed as I tread on it, walking past the
stand where the pitcher sits, and it is
that smell of fresh oily pesto,
or the smell of that great combination—tomatoes and basil—
that changes our lives when we first taste it.

But it is the huge bale of rosemary, also tied together, but
        fomenting out
into many directions, that dominates our autumn
rooms today.
Rosemary for remembrance,
the unforgettable smell
of roasted lamb, of scalloped potatoes,
of salt breads, of the medicine
of an herb garden, healing
our daily need for fragrance in
complex,
grown up
ways.

"Do you still wear perfume, Diane?"

"Do you still breathe, Terry?"

Of course. Beyond spring, summer, into autumn,
and finally in winter. Even over the ice
can you detect the slight subtle fragrance of Mitsouko?

Part IV. Braised Short Ribs

and purple mashed potatoes.
Violets. Well, I
altered that part of the recipe,
used normal white
Russet potatoes, mashed after the whole
day this savory bistro preparation had radiated its
autumn smell through the house. First
the ribs butchered into short blocks,
wide as the ceremoniously cut ribbon wrapping a new building,
were browned with olive oil,
darkened to the shade of old sunflower
heads, and then set aside
while the mirepoix,
—chopped celery, carrots, onion, garlic and shallots—
was sweated and just browned a little
in the same pot, then set to flambé
with brandy, only I used *Framboise*,
white raspberry brandy. And a cup of dry
red wine added and reduced by a third
before adding the beef stock and
the browned short ribs.
Then bring it all to a boil.
Into the oven, simmering, at a low temperature but not
so low that the pot would ever stop
simmering during its next three hours.
Now the aroma of the braised short ribs
rises in a puff and hovers through your hair,
around your ears, as you open the lid
and with tongs, remove the meat
to a platter. Now strain out the vegetables
from the juice, and put the juice in a bowl,
into the freezer to collect the fat.

Later, just before dinner
your *beurre manié*, soft and smooth
as baby skin is rolled into balls and whisked into the sautéed
    shallots
boiling now in more red wine to thicken into a sauce.

Set aside. In another pot you sauté
your already blanched pearl onions with oyster
mushrooms, crimini
mushrooms, shiitake
mushrooms, pieces of wild autumn.
Set aside.
Out of the freezer comes the cooking liquid with
a crust of fat thickly over its top. You cut
it off, discard, and ladle the jelled liquid
into your thickening sauce of wine and shallots and *beurre manié*,
bring it to boil and then reduce heat while allowing
it to continue to thicken. Add the braised ribs,
cook for about fifteen minutes, add the mushrooms and pearl
     onions,
and serve over mashed potatoes.

So simple this dish, but time consuming
to prepare. Yet its results are a house that is savory
all day, and a meal that has
a history of involvement.
A perfume that comforts daily reminders of our failures.

This is the perfume you cannot
wear everyday.
Not every day can generate
something so elaborate.
Cooking this meal to share with my husband, filling my house
with autumn's scent, makes me grateful
for our life together.
Later I fall asleep next to Robert with the
special unbottled fragrance of this autumn meal wafting
through the house. Burying my face in the
pillow, I locate the faint breath
of Mitsouko in the linen.
Am doubly thankful.

Yes, Terry.
I am sure I will always wear perfume.

Teacup Feet

responding to an image
from a Cathy Song poem

She said that bound feet
were so small
they could fit into teacups, and this was China where
everyone
drank tea. I wondered
if my own feet when I was young
would have fit into French breakfast *café au lait* bowls,
but I was in California.
Maybe Coke bottles should have been
the image?
And my mother drank her Maxwell House brew
from old cups that should have had
saucers, though they didn't have.
Perhaps they were left in North Dakota
where she started drinking coffee as a child
in her immigrant German shack?
And later
when I was a teenager,
she drank her many many cups of coffee each day
from stamped dimestore mugs, and her feet were so
misshapen from being poor and only wearing
ill-fitting shoes, that I wondered
what they had looked like when
she was a child.

Who puts these feet of little girls
into slippers shaped like teacups or coke bottles?
We girls ourselves cut them to size, trying to fit into fuck-me
Marilyn Monroe shoes, just like Cinderella's ugly
sisters, hacking off their toes to squelch bloodily into a tiny
glass slipper. Oh little worthless feet,

baby shoes,
baby shoes,
think of how they used to cast our
baby shoes into bronze,
put them on the table to remind us once
they loved us:
we were so helpless,
beautiful
and small.

II THE MIRAGE OF DESERT AND OCEAN

The Orange

Driving through the desert at night in summer
can be
like peeling an orange,
the windows rolled down, the prickly scent
of mesquite and sage
blowing through the car, the
perfume
of the twilight shadowed earth lingering;
the acrid spray of the peel,
with its meaty white pillow
nestles into your fingers.

You are driving from Los Angeles to Las Vegas,
running from your loneliness, an empty house,
an ocean which brings neither father nor lover.

For one hour, the wind streams through
your car, a
three-year-old Pontiac you have named Green Greed;
for one hour, the scent of all the desert
plants makes you feel
loved, makes you
forget you have no one
to talk to. You do not care about the
myth of the West, about
the City of Angels and its beaches.

You are not yet even slightly
interested in
gambling.
You are 32 and feel you have a destiny. Somehow
in that car,
on that night, alone on the wind-cooled highway between
    California

and Nevada, for one hour,
the fragrance of sage, especially,
made you complete,
moving swiftly over your face, through
nostrils, the car, you warm
from desert day fire.

You were not even looking
yet, for Beethoven in Las Vegas,
Snake Mother in the desert.
Your life was over, or
had not yet begun. Did you see
a map of Michigan filling your hand
as you peeled the big navel orange,
the one which glowed like fireflies
that wink
in Michigan summer nights?
The white membrane, the orange raindrop
textured meat of the fruit
saturating your hands with sugar
as you drive, as you drove,
as you remembered one
beginning?

from *Medea the Sorceress*

70

Image Is Narrative

a meditation on Francisco de Zurbaran's
Still Life: Lemons, Oranges, and a Rose

The lemons are for health and the sourness
of life, unless you understand it.
The tricks in life
are that nothing is hidden, only obscured
by desire, which makes us long
for what we do not have.

The oranges have their zest. Yet,
how pale they are. The
same color as the lemons, but with them are
leaves and stems and, of course,
some blossoms. Why
are orange blossoms
for weddings?
The lemon blossoms look and smell
the same. How
we choose
to obscure and misunderstand.

The rose is on a tray next
to a cup of coffee. Why
isn't this painting entitled, "Still Life:
Lemons, Oranges, Rose, and a Cup
of Coffee"?

Perhaps the cup
is empty
next to the fully blossomed rose? The oranges
take up the most space, even though
they are physically a bit smaller
than the lemons. That is because they are elevated

in a woven wicker basket, like a pedestal;
and the oranges are like an actress
on stage, with a wreath of fragrant star-white blossoms,
despite their pale lemon colour,
and their dainty roundness.

These facts assure me that in Spain
in the early 17th century, one painter, at least
wanted us to see
that even though he knew all
about it,
he wouldn't give away any of the
real secrets
of marriage.
But in this attentive scene,
this "still life,"
I for one read the empty cup,
the bloomed out rose,
those large lemons
—three as in fates or furies—
and find it not just for the contrast with
the pale yellow fruit
that the whole ground of the painting, including
the surface of the table
is black.

Sable wedding night in the garden
when the young bride is wearing her wreath of orange
        blossoms,
having been married to someone she's never met,
who now is drunk and pinching her breasts
like those oranges, those juicy
lemons, the rose from her hair,
fallen to the ground,
and there is only night ahead.
Bridal night
to be gotten through, now that the
guests are gone,
and all the cups empty.
I do not need a single human

in the picture
to tell me this story:
the lemons dominating the rose,
the oranges the color of lemons,
and the empty, not even named, bitter
cup of coffee.

from *The Rings of Saturn*

Braised Leeks & Framboise

for Annette Smith

The ocean
this morning
has tossed someone's garbage
over its surface,
half oranges
that make my mouth pucker for
fresh juice,
lettuce leaves
looking fragile, decorative, like scarves
for the white curling locks
of old water.
It is not hard
to think of Aphrodite
coming up out of the dense green,
fully formed but not
of flesh, of some tissue, floating
goddess–like
and pale.

For breakfast
one morning
you served fresh leeks, slender
as fingers from a sea goddess,
braised, with butter, delicate
from the Altadena garden.

It was at your house
that I first drank
that clear heady liqueur,
Framboise,
an *eau de vie*, promising
that fruit did not have to be

fresh-cheeked, fat or stupid,
that it could read Proust,
or learn differential
equations.
The Saturnian taste
of old raspberries, and the moon's
clear-fingered insistence
of leek. These two intangible things
I owe you,
along with—what? or
is there more?

The image of an onion, its sweet blanket layers.
The pebbled surface
of a raspberry.

from *The Rings of Saturn*
and *Emerald Ice*

Nell's Birthday

After the feast of Grandma's Tofu,
                Shrimps in Barbecue Sauce,
                Eggplant in Ginger Sauce,
                Smoked Pork and Dumplings,
                Beef with Broccoli,
and after the very European Strawberry Shortcake which L.W.
    made
and on which she placed
13 candles,
all of which you blew out in one breath,
and after Mark had given you the copy of Rhona Barrett's
How To Achieve Wealth and Sexual Ecstasy,
personally inscribed,
and Marilyn had given you some coupons
for free ice cream at Baskin-Robbins,
and after the more mundane things, and the bottles of wine,
and Jim's bottle of scotch,
and you had begun to smoke up the carton of Benson & Hedges
    Phyllis
brought you, and after Anita and Rob had left to go and listen to
the radio broadcast of John Ashbery's poetry reading,
and you had declared friendship for all,
and 10-year-old Sarah,
sweet little girl who cannot read, had seen Marilyn's
tortoise-shell comb in the shape of a shark and declared her
    passion
for it,

    then
        we left the Maple Gardens
            and went out into the night made cool
                only by trade winds;

to be driven home in Jim's large Oldsmobile.

The front seat was large enough for four. Jim was silent
as his car's push-button windows,
and the car was as large as Americans like to imagine all sharks.
You climbed into the back seat with your daughter, Sarah;
we drove home through neon Honolulu,
Jim quietly chauffeuring,
I, the visitor, trying to maintain my differences,
and not be absorbed into the landscape of Hawaii,
while you huddled in the back seat with your daughter,
so empty and quiet.

I am sure it was not the pain of 42 years creating your silence.
Rather, I felt as I once felt before,
that Death was the driver, taking us down Morning Street, down
Evening Street, through the silence of a gutted city.
I felt we drove into the River Styx.

Relieved to be let off at the Kaimana Beach Hotel,
like a reversal of the myth, I could not look back,
knowing that black car
with you huddled in the back seat, holding your sad daughter,
had a destination different from my own.
One you chose to go to.
And one from which you would not return.

Once up in my room, I sat on the balcony, watching the night's
        ocean,
thinking of you, as in the myth;
could any of us go where you are?
bargain for at least part
of your life?
To allow you, even, to appear yearly,
along with the narcissus,
the crocus, beautiful flower from which saffron is made,
and Wordsworth's daffodils?

Would this relieve at all that evening?
When you were in a large black car,
being driven in the music of silence,

                         no lyre,
                              no voices even,
surrounded by a city
of
drowned sailors?

            from *Cap of Darkness*

Grain

The midwest is a king-size package
of cereal.
Husks of wheat rustling into a bowl
like dry leaves in autumn,
the sound of field mice playing in the mushrooming dark
of an empty farmhouse kitchen.
                    And driving
to work in the seed of a car
in winter, snow crusting with its sugary lid
the bowl of warm meal, Michigan earth,
also home of asparagus and the square tomato, I see
the sun swathed in a flannel of snow,
a dim orange glow in the morning's sky
behind a bare-limbed tree.
                    PARIS,
I think,
                    at sunset,
but I was only once
in Paris
on a New Year's Eve, arriving at the Gare du Nord
from Salzburg, in Alpine snow,
the raw fingers of the waiter shucking oysters for us
in a cafe,
the traditional champagne/ I don't
remember
any sunrises,
but that scene, those ice-water reddened hands,
red as any California sunset,
the end of my marriage to a man who could not love women/ or
        was it
only
ME he could not love?
Winter comes every year, crusting over the stubbed grain fields,
here in the midwest

where, driving to work in the snow,
I sometimes think I am in
the city of Paris.
                    In summer
I look out my back windows into the oak trees,
and pretend that beyond
the back fence
is the Pacific Ocean.
                    Rustling leaves
make me
think I hear it. If there is so much beauty
in longing, surely it is hope then
that makes us happy,
not satisfaction.

My memory of Paris is filled with pain.
When I lived on the Pacific Ocean
also
(pain).
The object itself does not hold beauty;
nor the thought of it;
but the hope of what it might be.
A grain of wheat,
black earth,
the sun, like thick ice-water reddened hands
opening the New Year's Eve oysters.

from *The Rings of Saturn*

Viennese Coffee

Wearing a coat of whipped cream whiteness
drinking a steaming paper cup of coffee
waiting for a train in a station which unfolds and unfolds,
like a map on thick paper, crackling in our cold hands,

Wearing a long crow-black wool overcoat,
the hot coffee in its cardboard container
making steam rise out of your wet gloves,
is the only thing we share, you black, I white,
in our outer garments.

Beethoven wrote and wrote his black-noted
espresso rich sonatas and symphonies
in this city, and Mozart played zanily
as he rushed underground, but I ignored pain
in this city, and wonder now if Viktor Frankl and others
like Hitler didn't set in motion some axis
that requires all who come here to be able
to survive. Some the punishers and torturers,
others the receivers of pain. I, who had previously spoken
of betrayers, how could I have known
the scorpion "M" would betray me even while
we were visiting this city, I in the opera watching
La Bohème, he trailing young men
down the snowy streets even into the Austrian Alps.
The worst of betrayers, opening his body
like a tomb, making me wonder ever after if sex
were only for the depraved. Ah, city of Nazis, you offered
some answers to that question, didn't you?

The train stations hold fathers and mothers, also
with their paper cups of hot coffee,
and in my memory it is with a kind friend that I am standing,
as I leave for another city alone. He is the man

in the dark coat, and I visited him without
the snake coiling around my collar.
This coffee the only blackness.
Night a time for sleep,
the morning fresh as a star,
the paled out moon setting, and this evening
a Strauss opera, *Rosenkavalier*. Joy, love that is
shared, the only trickery results in fun.
I am an old fashioned woman,
not one who believes
that love and death go together.

from *Jason the Sailor*

The Fear of Fat Children

*upon the return of a much food-
stained copy of Bukowski's*
Dangling in the Tournefortia,
by a fat student

Age has blown me up like the wind spirit
of a Chinese river, whose
belly
hangs out over stylized waves, looking like the scales
of a carp. Ancient fish
with beveled fins swim up
from the past for crumbs carried in a greasy paper. That
must have been what was lying next to the book
you borrowed,
John, fat boy, with monster-face,
who sweats and smells like dirty socks
in our hot spring afternoon classroom. But it is age,
the approach of death, which has treated my body thus,
not birth, life, youth.
How these surfaces punish us,
yet when I ask myself which punishes more—
                          surface or interior—
I know
            I know
                          Can't
be satisfied.

Legally, we've just investigated Marilyn Monroe's death for signs
of murder, because we can't
just can't, believe she, with the luscious surface,
a melon, a lichee nut,
could have reason to kill herself.

And it is foolish of me to worry so

about your sweaty fat body, your fleshy bat-nose
flattened across your face, your smelly hands
which cannot allow you
to read a book without its looking as if you fried bacon
over it. Yet "fat"
has always been coupled with
"old" in my vocabulary.
And to me has always been a sign of
defeat.
                              I am afraid
of fat children,
of flesh in the young,
for it seems to be what death and the grave
are all about.
I am fat from drinking California cabernets,
eating *chèvres,* and crisp breads,
from *pâtés* and *pasta genovese,* cognac, butter,
vichyssoise, a summer of
tomatoes, an autumn of squash,
whereas you told me you ate packaged macaroni
dinners, and I am sure day-old doughnuts
and potato chips accompany every
page
you turn.

John, I wanted to give you
the Bukowski book
that summer day you returned it, greasy and limp,
but one look told me I couldn't,
for it would seem as if I were too prissy to handle
a dirty book,
belying my first instinct
which was to give you a gift of poetry.

There was my fear too,
of your young fatness,
and death.
I looked out the door
and did not see you,
but a mirror

of what I fear.
                 It is not
fat children,
but my own death, age.

The fat of wasted life.

from *The Rings of Saturn*

Salad Flowers

for Craig who provided these flower
meals in Bellflower and Malibu

The Pacific Ocean:
like a woman's skirt smoothed over
her lap. The sand, blown clean as the Sphinx,
is outside the window, and the black baby grand
with its white keys and these Malibu Canyon people,
some of whom are in this picture,
hold everything in place.

This is a scene
I am asking you
to close your eyes and
see.
Pretend you are a single lens
reflex, 35 mm,
and you are recording
this.

Arugula, cress, radicchio, some bibb,
dressed with balsamic vinegar. What is
on top? A bell. A yucca bell.
Its petals as thick as any magnolia lip,
and who would think to eat such flesh?
But its flavor is delicate
as the few grains of sand a child
sprinkled over the woman's naked toes.
Her hair, a strand of her hair loosed from the scarf
blows like the tinkling sand against her cheek,
and it is that delicacy, that almost only a tracing,
which she feels that is the
flavor of
the yucca blossom

we are eating;
which has garnished our
salads.

Could the scene be the same? Why not? This
ocean somewhere beyond the walls of this
cafe? No less in Bellflower, a real
town, than behind the oaks shading the fence at
the end of my backyard in Michigan? The
ocean is there, whether it is
California or Michigan.
And on this plate of
Belgian endive, of lobster as white
as the yucca bells and a tomato rose, its hushed
flesh almost hidden on the porcelain,
there are four pansies, two white and two
almost black. Oh, the velvet of the petals
should not be good to eat; oh, the velvet of their
cheeks should be for touching as the child
pats her mother's varnished red-tipped toes,
but those flowers too
end the meal
and I eat them.
I cannot believe they will taste good;
they will taste papery and dull,
but in fact
these pansies lie on my tongue
like melting sugar
of some exotic variety which does not burst
into instant sweetness, but instead slowly
seeps like a drowsy
moment
on the beach, with one
strand of your blond hair flowing
against your face, with the
child's round little hand
petting your tanned foot, and
the ocean, fluttering its white,
like a printed cotton skirt over your lap.

You are a woman
sitting on the beach.
This camera has focused
on a flower
which is like the ocean
the one remembered
or seen
which is always there. The
black piano playing
Debussy. Have I imagined this, about
eating flowers? Or is it the
woman or the
ocean or
even
the camera
which are imaginary? No,
I know
I tasted the flowers of yucca,
and I tasted pansies,
and the child was there
with her flower hand against my lacquered toes.

from *Medea the Sorceress*

Eating Flowers

I know that if you put your pencil
in a certain spot, it will
not rain there.

Then you
begin to draw the petals
of a rose.

There is moisture
on the real rose, but on this one
that you are sketching, every line
is dry as grandmother skin.

And when
you think of a salad
like young cousins, wet from swimming,
instead of a corsage in
the refrigerator;
when you remember the yucca bells
I mentioned once, floating
on top of a salad, across from the Blue
Pacific, not far
down the road from Annette's
white-domed house skimming on the cliffs
over Point Dume; then you will know
that drawing a thing in black and white is a better way
than eating it,
to own it.
Like a body left
in the desert, it can be preserved for
centuries.

I myself am against getting too dependent
on owning things. It's fear

that makes me think:
          the very bite I take
                    will turn into an albino serpent
                              or a parent in a hospital bed
                                        pure white, under my tongue.
But if I draw these
dry light powdery lines
that become a rose's petals, how
released I will
be.

I never thought I could stand
to lose someone I loved. But who
has a choice?

Open your eyes,
salty light, dry pencil sketches,
once consumed? Now
all *eau de vie* with–
drawn,
          rose petals in Wilton's gold desert bowl,
          a white-canopied mirage,
          a blue salad of lapis.

Had I
learned
to draw
rather than eat, I am sure
that I would have found less
anguish in my life. This is not to say
that if you put your pencil
in a certain spot,
even if it does not rain there,
that you will not get wet.

Violets

cups of them,
the wet bank, earth cressed,
roots exposed in the cutaway grainy
crust

water tears at the edges,
but the violets on the bank
near a tree are firm,
not fragile, even resist sometimes
the crushing of a foot, springing back
as if they could not so easily be
torn or pressed away.

The candied violets with which I've
adorned chocolate glazed tortes
stay fresh for years. So that we forget
it was not the sweet which we sugared them for,
but age. The natural taste of violets
or pansies reminding your mouth of hummingbird life
bee genes, ant activity, spilled honey.

The big man said to us he didn't know if he'd like
eating flowers. I smiled to myself, thinking
that he'd probably eaten hundreds
and not known it. Anyone who drinks tea,
has drunk flowers; pea pods often flourish the vestige
of the white flower at their tips; the world is studded
with rose petals, jasmine, chamomile, saffron,
nasturtium. Surely these petals or stamen
have passed his lips some time.

I think he must have had a image of a cattleya
massively presented, like a steak on his plate. Or a giant
lily being offered in someone's hand, to hold and crunch on.

The smallness of so many flowers, edible and otherwise,
might be another reason we don't think of them.
So interesting, then, that this tiny one,
the violet,
commands notice:
La Traviata,
The Fallen Women,
or the trivial one,
the small one. Her name is
Violetta. How can we forget her
as we sing her name?

from *The Emerald City of Las Vegas*

Pamela's Green Tomato Pie

She stands by the sink
her feet neat and white,
her slim arms rolling the pie crust
and deftly arranging it in the pan so that
she can fill the cavity with
paper-thin
sliced
green tomatoes.

I am sitting in the carpeted room beyond the sink,
sipping a glass of burgundy,
talking to her husband, and watching her
as she clicks through the action,
glancing occasionally at the thick volume of *Gourmet*
then sprinkling brown sugar into the swirl of tomato slices,
glancing again at the cookbook, continuing to
make small motions from which my attention wanders,
finally fitting the top crust on, with precision,
neatly made, a package compact and delectable, to be placed in
    the oven.

The woman who is making the green tomato pie
is a strange woman. She speaks English
as if it were a foreign language to her,
but we all know it is not.
It sometimes makes me feel as if she is from another planet,
or a robot or android,
programmed to be the perfect woman,
so beautiful and graceful,
intelligent and talented,
yet somehow,
none of those things quite meshing.
Unlike many beautiful women, she
does not make you gasp when

you see her slender body, clear eyes, blond hair
appear.
     Nor do her talents seem very extraordinary
     when you are faced with her life;
     she is the kind of good dancer who makes
     a perfect partner, but whom no one notices,
     perhaps for her very grace,
     when she dances.

I sit there sipping my burgundy, asking myself
where the puzzle of this woman is,
that she should be special in so many ways,
yet nothing quite fits together,
none of it adds up to "extraordinary human being," something we
    all
call her husband
whose talents when separately enumerated
do not sound like so many as hers.

And she is a troubling friend to have;
she is so unhappy, and does not seem ever to fit properly into any
    life.
Yet, all that grace. And in spite of it,
I find myself often quarreling with her, or preaching.
She leaves me so exasperated.

Like a button, just too large for the hole, the only one you could
    find
to sew on yr blouse which makes the whole front look lumpy but
which was the only button in the house even close to the size you
needed, and you couldn't go to work without sewing it on unless
    you
chose to use a safety pin.
She doesn't quite fit.

Yet, when she serves the green tomato pie,
its unusual flavor and delicate textures make even
the non-pie eaters at the table
—like me—
murmur with appreciation and pleasure.

94

Her ten-year-old son eats two helpings. And he's a good kid, but
      not
really
a child gourmet.
So, here was something perfect she did,
her husband usually being the cook,
and it seemed quite exquisite,
like all of her life should be.
Yet no one remembered to tell her how exceptional it was when
      we left that evening,
though cooks in our crowd are always praised
for their special efforts.

It should have changed her image.
She should have become
the perfectly carved bone button, matching all the others
on the blouse.
But
even in my mind
she has not.
Even in retrospect, I think of the green tomato pie
as something not quite fitting in,
though it was so exceptional, it should not have been required to
fit in.

The pie was perfect, almost unnoticed, a moment in her life,
and I do not know why,
but she will not have many

such moments.

from *Cap of Darkness*

Whole Sum

The swimming pool/turquoise water
white rings of light undulating
on the surface,
each ring plunging down, rotating,
hula hoops of water-light appearing and disappearing
as the white-capped swimmers lap
the pool.

July
and I need to change my life
which tastes of shimmering red heaps of sliced
tomatoes
and translucent white slices of onion,
the picnic worship of salt,
the fruity granulation of sugared teeth.
Food in hampers,
sticky potato salad, tins of crisps,
buns, pickles which linger in vinegar,
cheeses which ferment and ripen in dark corners.

My vision of firm brown bodies,
curly heads,
shoulders dripping in jeweled elegance
from the swimming pool is this:
a frosty drink in hand,
the mouth ready for a summer feast.

Death,
disease, decay,
shoved into the mouth. Each bite
an attack on the liver. Each
sip an assault on the kidney. Shoveling
picnic food into rubbery young bodies,
filling them with bites and

sips of death.
We are eating, eating,
summer pleasure,
summer joy,
summer death.

We eat in communion with waste/   ALL we
eat is mud. The
swamp fills our mouth.

I sit this July morning
overlooking the turquoise water
undulating around the smooth brown swimmers.
They are fighting death,
while I walk willingly to my scrubbed
morning table,
willing to bite flaky croissants,
swallow gold butter,
taste a perfect egg (once a life's beginning),
drink mythic tea,
and know each beauty, each
pleasurable sensation
is my death.
My death from food,
as all death comes,
beautiful and terrible,
out of life.

from *The Magician's Feastletters*

Pears

Of chutney, and poaching, of hard
   brown Boscs, and the foxy Red, of
      Comice in a padded box, some even
with foil as golden as Moronai
   blowing his trumpet over Utah.
      The tabernacle of autumn fruit
is not a place where
   everyone can worship,
      the whisper of apple breath
can't always be heard,
   the dusty grapes piled in wagons
      on their way to the winery don't always
appear at tables where there are hungry
   people, in fact
      the beauty of fruit
is not often consumed by the poor,
   but the rich have it there
      on platters,
to ignore. "My dear," they might say
   to a stranger, "have some fruit,"
      but we know that a perfect pear
in a tart, or a Belle Hélène, a melba
   or in a still life painting
      is the opposite of asphodel.
We know the details of
   peeling, and rending the
      soft core.

Human History: Its Documents

Sometimes poison
a decoration
in our lives/ or more.

                            Black oily
French Roast
coffee beans, ground and brewed,
steaming in a cup/ the day still with no wasted and empty
words
in it,
      thick cream
floating on the beverage,
the memory of a silver pot and a silk coverlet
somewhere behind
this desirable poison,

hot from the oven
flaky butter dough, a beautiful parchment
croissant,
the fingers covered with a film
of grease,
the flour milled empty of
nurture,
appeasing the eye and tongue, like
delicate crumpled stiff letters
in the belly,
the cream which would bloat the stomachs of
African children/ we have evolved too far
to digest it,
these poisons ARE TREATS
to start special mornings, as if
I were the woman in
the peignoir
on "Sunday Morning,"

listening for the beat of giant bird wings,
pterodactyl,
the big poetic line
I wait for
with these poisons I long for.

Spring coming and I fantasize Hot Cross Buns,
all of civilization summed up
in dough,
bean,
viney resins,
and the paper, the ink
which allows us to transmit
our recipes,
I, standing in line to do my monthly banking
watch a young pregnant mother lean over to her two-year-old
and stuff into his unwilling mouth
a piece of candy. She is grinning and nodding, as if she were in a
Punch and Judy show. "Good," she is saying, as the child grimaces
        and
drools and finally chews his little pellet of poison sugar. She
beams
to us all,
as we stand in line with checks and bills. How good she believes
herself to be, having just begun one young child's craving
for poison. Food
that will never nourish
and, in this case, didn't even
please.

Yes, how I hated that school teacher's phrase, "You can trap more
        flies
with honey than with vinegar." As if we were all going out there
to read *Song of Myself* and *Howl*
to a large swarm of irritating flies.

from *The Magician's Feastletters*

Orphée

Eating Greek food,
grape leaves stuffed with rice and lamb,
moussaka with eggplant bursting out of nutmeg and oregano,
drinking retsina,
I think of my friend, Robert Kelly,
of my reluctance to control myself
yet my anger at chaos.
Clint stands to my left,
Kelly on my right.
We each hold
scrupulous regard
for perfect food
and appropriate drink.
Victims of our bodies
we have followed our imagination's
exclusive hunt
      Clint betrayed by
            Clotho who spun a dissolving threaded tapestry,
    Kelly by
            Lachesis who assigned him a starving man's destiny,
    and I, by myself,
            Atropos, the scissors,
            the cutting mouth, uttering
            the syllables,
            not wanting to control,
            only mouthing
a frame
to perfectly surround
a certain world,
and only the bather's foot
stepping on to
the beach,
all else cut off.

Scissors,
framer,
each picture still,

and so perfect, like
Eurydice whom
we can never
bring back.

from *The Magician's Feastletters*

Using Heather's Wooden Spoon

clear the air for winter,
breathe in, for some never give up!

From the black beans, with onions
sliced like crescent moons,
and celery chopped
into comet trails, and morsels of pepper bacon
ruffled Mars brown, the soup
is telescoping into the kitchen a message
of galactic pleasure. I am
calling the Silver Surfer home,
not waiting for his itinerant moment,
instead sending this aromatic
mist out into the lens of space.

Black Bean Soup will open its
spicy mouth
and say hello to any cosmic
traveller.

. . .

The black bean soup is not to everyone's taste. I find it reminds
me of a Spanish world I often envy, one with the zest of flamenco
dancers, and the chili of fringed eye lashes. Growing up in
Southern California put adobe in my blood, along with silver
bridles and belt buckles, and the heavily tooled leather that
caballeros flaunted on horseback in the Rose Parade.

Wakoski's Petunias★

Ruffled skirts

How we applauded
Sylvia Estrada's flamenco dancing

in Southern California
8th grade.
                She
was not a Mexican,
she said,
        but Spanish/ her father
owned an
orange grove.
Childhood bigotry/ all
we knew,
that some were better than us,
and a few not.
How important those last few,
as we sat on
the sagging screened porch
knowing we had nothing
but our whiteness
and the bank
did not even give credit for that.
I was plump and tired
at 13,
but Sylvia Estrada was a thin hot wire
of brown magnetism. Like a
stick
in her ruffled skirts
and rhythm, thinness, make-up, curls,
money
I would never have.

How we applauded.
I still think longingly
of the flamenco clatter and pistol fire
on the old Washington School
Auditorium floor.

.   .   .

Wilton, my genius friend who was adopted into an upper middle
class, happy North Carolina family, his father a Reynolds Tobacco
executive; Wilton with his degree from Oxford and his three
successfully published novels, still under forty but no kid any more;

Wilton, when I ask him, "Don't you ever want to meet your birth mother or at least know who she was?" says

"Why?
Why should I?"

I am silent, but then can't help saying, "Just to satisfy your
    curiosity? Just to know?" I could say so much more, but bury
    it. Silence it.

"I can't think of any reason why I'd want to know," he says.

.   .   .

Yes.
        My own mouth has been calibrated
against measuring
the past
for so long, surely
there is no galaxy I can locate,
no earthy black bean soup
for dipping the hard crusted bread,
no flamenco buzz of exotic puree, scented
with lemon juice
and infused with some sherry,
to offer me now
any other soup that the one I have cooked,
the black bean soup, stirred with Heather's wooden spoon
surprising me always with
the delicate taste that comes from such
a crude earth-bound protein.

        * the portion of this poem called "Wakoski's Petunias"
        is from *The Rings of Saturn*

Breakfast at George & Molly Wickes'

The checked cloth,
the muffins,
and the tea. The marmalade
and jams
                in the woodsy edge
of an Oregon town
telling me
morning is a time
I need to get
acquainted with.
I associated it with fatigue,
days I wish did not have to be lived through,
not accomplishment
but endurance.

This, my own attitude
of impatient forbearance,
New England
not in my blood,
the West, dust, the desert of another day.
How I want to rise each morning,
overlook the Pacific,
drink my tea with a view
Balboa might have had.

At your table
morning itself, apart from landscape,
presented fingers and toes,
the cream new with possibilities,
the jams, not death (poison sugar)
but just the right
sweetening for a day. Was John Cage joking
when he said
there's just the right amount

of evil in the world?
If only I could perceive that Truth
and find each morning
new and clear
as Jeffers' view of our western
ocean.

.   .   .

And my memory of the pacific
clear
tree-filled morning
with breakfast at your satisfying
table.

from *The Rings of Saturn*

George Washington's Autumn

Could he have seen flashes
of the boardwalk at Atlantic City,
September 1983,
the beach like a beautiful well-formed mouth,
not smiling but solemnly inviting
one into the ocean
which is black and forever, no thought of
ships or sailboats, no swimmers alive,
a place where the dead join
the other waste of civilization?

These mornings when it is cool and
the orange umbrellas are
not yet up,
the sand white, shaded with charcoal,
your face and mine,
familiar behind hot paper cups of coffee and tea.

from *The Rings of Saturn*

III   *A California Girl Moves to Michigan via New York City*

The Coffee Drinker

for Carol Bergé

When I was as new feeling as salamander skin,
when my young feet were daikon radish flesh,
and my eyes used to bare dusty floors and plastic dishes,
I saw your Lower East Side apartment in New York, five
    flights/no
elevator, up,
not as poverty,
but like an expensive old trunk
filled with glass beads, woven textures from China,
or Belgium, silver trinkets, carved wood,
bits of Kalims. Nothing you had
was new, but everything was
from an exotic place, as if it had been owned by a parrot.
The kitchen had bent, once-costly copper pots,
hand-thrown crockery, wooden implements stained and scrubbed
with use. There were a million different woods in all
the furnitures, pictures covering every inch of the old walls,
lovely bits of cloth to walk on, splashes of red in the
umber rooms. In each chamber, there was evidence of
daily living. Half a peach saved and resting on the sink,
a yellow plate with three fourths of a knish covered with
waxed paper and half a cup of that black cinnamon-y Mexican
    coffee
in a thick cup, sitting there neatly, not as if it had been
left for washing up, but for its actual purpose:
to be drunk later when you felt like
finishing it.

Scenes of contrasting beauty plague us all
as we wait for the alchemy that will offer transformation.
It was that saved,
unfinished

cup of coffee
sitting on my own kitchen sink this morning
which made me think
of the half-eaten peach
and our different lives.
The empty sweep of my rigid world,
bare surfaces
and desert maps
where one mouthful,
one drop,
one teaspoon, of water—
could not make a difference,
would be lost or not counted in the
desolate landscape. Contrasted
with how you
have always rescued old things
for one inch of the velvet which still has its nap
or saved a little of the coffee
in case one mouthful of its rich oils
might revive you in an afternoon of rejections
or failures.

from *Medea the Sorceress*

Letter with the Ring of Truth

Dear Clayton,
                    In bushel baskets, the yellow pears
bruise each other's bodies with ripeness.
I imagine the late summer pear
orchards of France
because, like most Americans
I think that beauty originates
in Europe,
and I would rather eat Stilton Cheese
than Wisconsin Blue. We say,
"as American as apple pie,"
and count Johnny Appleseed
among our folk heroes,
yet the most delicious Granny Smith
apples I ever ate
found in the Atlanta farmer's market one winter,
were from France,
bearing little round labels depicting the Eiffel Tower,
cracking like rifle shots when
you bit into them, tart
against the English Stilton
or French boucheron.

Emily, Walt, Wallace, Robinson,
all ate American
and never set foot off this continent
except Jeffers who yielded finally in middle age to his wife's
        longing
for Europe.

I chide you, my friend, for exploring
the caves of the Dordogne
rather than meandering on the American continent.
Comparing myself to the fat native

palm trees of Southern California
I say I know
my roots,
my American fathers,
and claim my native speech,
but now as I wander in the early autumn–late summer
farmer's market,
I go hunting for Italian tomatoes,
European cucumbers,
herbs like basil for making pesto,
herbs like tarragon
which grows in French gardens
and which Americans use without imagination.
I want rosemary for my lamb,
a meat few Americans understand,
and while everyone else is ordering his Thanksgiving turkey,
I put in my order
for a goose.

California's wines
I still claim over burgundies
or the fruits of the Côtes du Rhône,
but I reject bourbon or sour mash
whiskey, preferring Scotch or
Irish, and usually prepare
tortes rather than cobblers or pies
when I entertain.
Where do our roots start?
In what we eat,
or what we read? As a
child I was okay. If you asked me what my favorite foods were
without hesitation I'd say,
     "corn on the cob"
     "watermelon"
     "ice cream". But now
I can go whole years without consuming
any of them.
And when I dream of eating,
it is of *chèvres*,
French bread,

114

Granny Smith apples from the Pyrenees,
extra virgin
olive oil, fresh basil
and garlic, with imported pasta.

Walt, Emily, how did you resist
these things, maintain
your truth?

The Pacific pounds
at my white, aging feet. I
listen for the voice which belongs
to this shore
and no other. Why do I hear this
melange of sound?
Now I am walking in the
Michigan farmer's market.
standing near this bushel basket
of yellow Bartlett Pears, grown right here
in a nearby orchard.
The orchard is heavy with
the hum of bees. No one
here has heard of Poire William
or any other *eau de vie*, though I'm
told some locals, not the Calvinists because they are teetotalers,
prepare a potent homemade brew from the
windfalls, a pear cider. As
yet, I haven't tracked it down,
but I wait, remembering my first trip to Michigan
when an English professor who can actually transplant,
    successfully,
Michigan wildflowers into his garden
served me
Cherry Bounce,
homemade Michigan liqueur.

What is a native American?
Someone who believes in corn?
The "corn-porn lyric"?
Or one who can reconcile everything

because he has such a big map
in his head?

This meander I write to you, Clayton,
who are from Indiana,
heart of the North American continent.
I post it from Michigan, my residence
to California, my home.
Your home.
At least we know where we stand
no matter
how deeply
or diversely
our roots extend.

from *The Rings of Saturn*

A Californian Fights Against the Old New England Traditions

to Stanley Kunitz

The elderly famous man goes shopping with
me at the Safeway
and while I am filling my cart with the
most interesting cheeses
I can find
(alas, not many)
and searching for good mustard and other
exotics,
I see him
in his sailor's cap and small
safari jacketed shoulders
bending over the margarines, comparing
prices, looking for sales;
we move together to the coffee aisle,
and while I spot the Colombian
—in a can—lament
that our vacation house does not have a
coffee grinder,
feel complacent that I have
brought my own teapot and can of
Fortnum & Mason Ceylon Tea,
I notice that he is peering at all the prices,
and finally choosing the can of coffee whose price
is the most spare,
Edwards Brothers.

We move over to soups,
and I finally get tired of watching.
Rebelliously, youthfully (tho I am forty), I say,
"No wonder I will never get rich. I can't bear all this comparing."

117

During the week, I discover that he cooks well,
though I hate losing supremacy in the kitchen. Yet,
his thirty years of seniority makes me feel
like withdrawing over
and over again.

When he reads manuscripts,
I think of his small figure bent over the Safeway prices,
comparing, looking for the most economical.
I ask myself whether my values represent only the wastrel,
his, the efficient?

No answer. But an understanding of what
constitutes extravagance.
If I spend too much, then
by the same token I think, he spends
too little.

Now, I have to condemn myself, though,
for looking at a frail old-man's life
and letting my own gimlet eyes
give him so little.

"Where is your extravagance now, Westerner?" I ask myself.
"Who is being stingy, giving up excellence
in favor of bargains?"

Ashamed of my own lack of generosity
still I must hold the accusation, meanly.
A young Californian rebelling against New England,
knowing my origins are from hot countries,
lands unlike Massachusetts or New York. Lands
where the huge mountains
are deeply packed with precious minerals,
even gold.

Where everything is big,
with the space of the desert,
big, like I want to be.

from *Cap of Darkness*

Clint's Bottle of 1977
Châteauneuf-du-Pape

Robert bought a finch feeder &
immediately attracted
two finches.
I played my computer blackjack game
all day.
There was sun on
the snow.
Clint came at 7 wearing his
outrageous T-shirt.

We had New England Boiled Dinner
and drank
the CNdP.

from *The Rings of Saturn*

Eggs

"The perfect food," says
Carlton Fredricks "(if you can eat them)."

Their smooth selves like Sahara sand rills,
or the duvet on Heidi's loft bed in the Alps,
or the hands which smoke calla lily cigarettes cold
from Norman's orchid freezer, offer
a mouth closed, invisible
to even Cooper's Hawkeye. The mute parts
of our country, like the egg.
The Great Plains, so smooth in March as we drive
through Nebraska to the edge of the high desert
of Colorado.

In Crete, Nebraska, Greg Kuzma goes
to the Athens Bar and Grill, like Hemingway, to eat
the $1.99 eggs and coffee special breakfast
and then write poems for an hour or two. Some artists
want studios on the coast of Maine or California,
or in the densely textured woods of birches and mending walls.
But Greg has grain elevators at his back,
and the midwestern road which unrolls like a long tongue
that cannot form words, only long, long
humming sounds.

He knows something I can only
guess, as we drive the road
and see the few trees which stand out like the Statue of Liberty,
marking farms or settlements. They are so clearly limned
against the March
sky that I can see each hawk's nest,
most of them with a Red Shouldered
or is it a Swainson's
focused in the thin-lit trees?
American birds, but not turkeys.

120

Hawks, probably with eggs in those nests. Me, the Californian,
the dull unnoticed daughter of Jeffers whizzing by, but
what he notices,
the driver of this hot steel car,
what he saw on these Great Plains was
the egg of grain elevators,
the smooth face with the mouth pinched in,
not to speak but to hold inside
the truth of wheat.

I, who love American breakfasts of bacon, eggs, and toast, I
worship these birds which cross the entire face
of our continent,
though
I do not think their lives
superior to human lives. They pose a riddle:
what speech is silent
and thus can say the most?

If I made a triptych
holding Madonna Liberty,
Elvis with the face of an American hawk,
and the King of Spain wearing his cap of darkness,
I would reveal my Trinity.
And I would have to wonder if the chapel-shape
which framed our portrait-selves
would not be
the egg-smooth monoliths of Nebraska's
grain elevators?
This shape shifting vision,
a gift from the driver
who wears the photographer's cap of invisibility,
whose voice is in his eye,
not a mote,
but a kernel of wheat,
the entire act of piety, to breathe,
to eat, finally,
to see: America's
beginning
in her grain-y
elevated eggs.

The Pumpkin Pie, Or Reassurances Are Always False; Though We Love Them, Only Physics Counts

Pumpkin,
freshly scraped out of its tightly adhering
orange skin,
as if you tried to scrape
beach foam off the sand,
the seeds washed and set out for the birds on the porch,
churned in the blender, after baking to watery
pulp in the oven.
                                        Fresh
pumpkin,
in other words,
not that bright yellow stuff
that comes in tins,
and ready to make pie.

Enter this cook:
the experienced artist who grew up
with tin cans and a cupboard with only two
spices—salt and cinnamon.
It is my first time to make a pumpkin pie
from pumpkin.
The tin can being so much cheaper,
the time required, so much less.

How do I say this:
        cooking smells,
        as the flaky crust is baked,
        and I am stirring the custard filling,
         pumpkin pulp,
         cinnamon (my spice),
         nutmeg,

       ginger,
       allspice,
       cloves,
       the delicious thick cream,
       sugar,
       eggs,
       oh good things, and I am
stirring, stirring, not allowing
any lumps,
the spices wafting out into the house and
feeling the perfume of the kitchen,
thinking that men make better cooks than women
because they have ideas about what they do,
not feeling the simple urge to fill up or provide
a meal,
stirring, stirring, thinking
wondering what a man I love is doing,
thinking of different kinds of skills, thinking
also
of a poet who writes about music and water together,
stirring and wondering,
wondering
why this custard does not get thick,

and finally the correct amount of time being passed,
and the custard seeming thicker but not as thick
as I think it should be and knowing that
when custard starts to get thick
it gets thick really fast,
right away,
so hastily, with Mercury whizzing around my heels,
I pour it into the pie shell,
then think with horror, what?
if it doesn't
get thick?
And it is an hour from dinner,
lots of guests,
and not enough cream to do the whole thing again.

I wait.

Women know about waiting.
Artists know about waiting.
Lovers are the only ones who never learn
about waiting.
But even they often
have to wait.
"Please tell love to wait for me,"
says one of the great poets,
but love never waits for anybody, at least
not in the rain,
oh tears,
oh metaphors.

Anyway,
I wait.
Test the pie filling with a knife.
Not a silver one,
because this house has no silver,
I have never had silver,
but test it,
no good.
It still isn't firm.
I put it in the refrigerator.

I wait.
I take it out after anxiously waiting,
which means I didn't wait very long.
Oh, this perfect gourmet's delight,
something even the pilgrims seemed to be able to whip up,
and I in this modern house
worrying and wondering,
has poetry really informed my life?

I have not been waiting long enough.
Anxiously, I say to a lady who has been hovering around
the kitchen,
                "do you think it will set?"
She looks reassuringly,
as you would look at a child who wants to know
if daylight will come again,

a lady whose husband has said that pumpkin pie
is his favorite.
                    (did his mother use pumpkin out of the can?)
I now think I should have strained my
homemade pumpkin pulp through a jelly bag to get out
excess water
                    oh techniques,
how they do us in.

Reassuringly, my catechism is answered:
                    will the pumpkin set?
                              of course
                    do you think it will be okay by dinner?
                              of course, it will be delicious.

Of course.
Dinner. A menu I will not describe. Delicious.
Preceded by many drinks, many
appetizers, accompanied by much wine,
much laughter and flirtation,
a party occasion.

THE PUMPKIN HAS SET

The pie disappears from plates. Says
my reassurer,
the lady who holds the catechism,
the one whose husband's favorite was
Pumpkin Pie,
"I didn't think it would set.
But it turned out perfectly."

Stunned,
I smile my Christmas smile at her.
I have spent the last month thinking of that.
Why did she tell me she thought the custard would set,
if she didn't think it would?

Hateful.
I am a child.

We are all children. To be reassured.
I am ready to make her my enemy.

I have been duped.
Treated as a fraud
or lied to,
de-frauded.
Religion is dead: if there is no truth in the kitchen
where could there be truth?
                              I expect
a betrayer in the bedroom, perhaps,
or in any other room of the house,
the helpless mechanic under the car in the garage,
the sad plumber in the bathroom,
even a hopeless fire builder or clumsy handyman.
But not in the kitchen.

Women are true.
Faithful.
Honest.
Poets
speaking
committed words
through their small lives.

That was last Christmas.
I live this year
in one room,
have no kitchen,
garage,
fireplace or
bedroom.
I even share my bathroom.
Truth is lonely and unbetrayed.

I think of the motherly woman who lied, kindly, last year,
thinking to reassure me;
wonder now at my anger,
think how easy it is to condemn,
how hard to be compassionate.

What I know is that
I have always lived alone
with my own pumpkin pie truth.

And poetry,
the reassurer,
                    "Do you think it will set?"
        "Of course,
        it will be delicious."

                    from *Emerald Ice*

Apricot Poem

for Bob

Mother sits on a painted white chair in the kitchen.
Her apron is filled with apricots.
She cuts and pits them for jam.
When the fruit cooks with sugar and pineapple, the kitchen
    steams.
The wooden spoon gets shiny and sticky as it stirs.
The fragrance of jam clings to my ears and fingers.

. . .

Sitting
alone
my feelings turn to apricots, piled in my hands.
Their flesh:
like
it is living—yours. The apricots are feelings
in my hand.

Two kinds of jam—one for company and one for everyday.
The mixture bubbles
and the hornets hang about the back porch screen
trying to get in.

When you are gone
I balance each fruit on the back of my fingers,
flex my hand against their soft weight.
I wait

for you. I take each apricot, separately.
I make a line of them on the wooden table.
I touch each one with a fingertip
so that
my hand is extended

palm down
and slightly cupped
to touch one apricot with each finger.
I listen for footsteps.
I look in the mirror for any signs of snow.
I remember your hand on mine,
cupping mine entirely.

I put the apricots in a bowl,
but I hold one in my hand when I go to sleep,
because of the way it feels.

Could the jam have made my cheeks soft?
It is in that kitchen of twenty years ago.
I dream and dream, waiting for you;
when you come home
I will be sleeping.
In my hands children dance;
they throw apricots for balls.

from *Discrepancies & Apparitions*
and *Trilogy*

What Would Tennessee Williams
Have Said

Is there drama in everyday life?
I wonder
as I boil the water for my
morning tea.
The tea has stained
the white porcelain parts of the pot so that they look
like the feathers of a sparrow. I scrub,
but the crazed surface
inside
bares its old horse teeth at me,
impossible with stain.

The half dozen evening grosbeaks
flying up in yellow and black flurry,
as if someone has torn the business pages
out of the phone directory and thrown
them up in the air,
flying from the asphalt pavement
of the woodsy road we were driving,
the surprise of their beauty,
their unfamiliarity, like seeing the hundreds
of small purple wild iris
along the same road, for the first time.
Also startling.
Exciting.
But were those moments
dramatic?
Or the most dramatic events
that happen in my daily life? What
would Tennessee Williams have said,
I wonder, about the last poetry program
I was asked to give?

When the director wanted me to wear
a cape and
invited me to a dinner party in his kitchen
where we ate with his senile mother, victim of Alzheimer's
disease. No
> drinks were offered but
> herb tea. He
> was making cheddar cheese soup
> out of plastic bottle of something processed,
> and his mother would say things like,
> "I'm hungry, I want some bingbang now,"
> and
> "I saw her coming out of the refrigerator
> with a nogger and she birded it,"
> and, flaring up with anger,
> "You'd better give me some more to eat, or I'll
> cruise!"
The aging house they lived in was stacked with newspapers,
and he ironed his
trousers while we waited for the nurse
to come and stay with his mother.
When we got to the theater
there were only six
people
in the audience. I wore the cape
for a while,
but it jingled and was hot.
It was a beautiful
garment, a sculpture
really, but not made for giving
poetry readings.

The director told me at length how
he cares for his senile mother,
who is incontinent and who eats
everything she finds, like a baby. We saw
this at dinner, as she kept chewing
parts of her paper napkin.

How can you not admire

a man who will stay at home
and care for a senile mother; yet
how can you not hate him
for inviting you to dinner, a celebration for a
performance/you are nervous, in a strange place
not knowing who will be there/
with his senile mother,
eating in the kitchen, while he irons
his trousers,
with neither alcohol, caffeine nor festive food to
alleviate the tension. A pretense
that we are not strangers, or have a friendship
that does not exist?

Where is the drama,
or poetry?
I see only
humiliation,
and my own sense of meanness
that the whole night angered me,
and reduced me
to these petty observations.
What would Tennessee Williams have said
about that evening?
That you can turn anything trivial
into art? What do I say
about it?

That I was humiliated?
Made aware of the foolishness or parsimony
of my own life?
That for the past two months
I have felt over and over
how demeaning it is
to resent being asked to dinner in a kitchen
with a senile stranger?

Yet I see her,
again and again,
in her blue cotton shirtwaist dress,

eating her paper napkin,
speaking like a mad child,
and her son, who wiped our plates, as well as hers,
with the pink sponge between soup and salad,
scrubbing down his mother's dress after the meal
with the same sponge, pink
on her baby blue dress.

Robert and I escaped finally to the yard,
he smoking,
I wondering
what vision of myself,
the future,
this event was supposed to make me take
away?
Wondering what Tennessee Williams would have done,
or if some things really are
too petty or mean
or cruel
for life. Whereas art can
absorb everything?

Some animals, like foxes,
kill the old when they are no longer cunning enough
to survive alone.

from *The Rings of Saturn*

Sue's Diet

for Sue Walker

A tiny can
of tuna
and a glass of wine.

Lunch.

Snowing here
but sun through the live oaks where
she is. I am wearing
my polar bear sweater,
creamy against the snow,
my body shaggy with
winter fat.

Dinner
she skipped.
And turned into a
silkie.

She is beautiful
with Titian hair and
creamy arms, whereas I'm a woman
who would not look good unless
I were thin and had a tan.

Even then
no man dreams of me

Perhaps that's why
they offer other gifts.
They think I might be enchanted,.
When they understand

polar bears and silkies
we will both undress for them.

Until then,
where's the magic?

Under the snow? As the fat melts
from our bodies?

Gabriella's Influence on Our Vision of Plato's Cave

When she rolls a cigarette, it is
like the Looking Glass River at dusk,
Robert fishing for pike,
a Kingfisher with its mad blue lightning bolt crest
diving, and me at home, thinking
how nice it is that Robert
can go fishing while I read and drink wine. He can
order his life in the flat-bottomed boat
as I order mine in the kitchen
filled with copper and Portuguese tiles. Gabriella
isn't someone we'd choose
to be friends with, but
a philosopher on his way to Paris
sees her as one of those blue packages of Gauloise,
the cigarette for people with strong lungs. In fact, I am
surprised that Gabriella doesn't smoke them,
Gauloise bleu, but when she rolls her own cigarettes
she reminds me of the local river
which is not beautiful except in name,
or to us with no other choice, no other close place to go, and
    then
its name, almost Cooper-ian, old American,
as in "Glimmerglass," a reminder of wildernesses
that no longer exist, of deep and clear waters
that have been transformed.

When she rolls a cigarette,
this woman who was so rude to us, she reminds me
that she too looks better at dusk, and only
if you don't have the waters of the Iroquois Nation
to compare to the Looking Glass River.
And Robert finds peace fishing there with his friends,

or alone, the way she does
when she leaves the table, finds a quiet isolated place
to smoke, rolls a cigarette from the dainty makings
in a little plastic baggy. American. Is she thinking of cowboys,
the West, she from a third world country?

I like the man who loves her, like him despite the fact
that he has no use for Plato, to me the cornerstone
of thought,
and I think of them, when she rolls a cigarette,
and I find myself thinking of Robert's Looking Glass River,
the compromises we all make to lead acceptable lives,
not to die from our own past excesses and dangerous desires.
How what we see reflected on the wall of the cave
is sometimes the only remnant
of a blue Gauloise package, empty of cigarettes,
though how can we know
from only the shadow?

Lunch with Miriam & Toby

for Miriam Olson

Bielo Polje means
White Field.

Miriam, I think of you
with your mouth of dressed petals
saying to me that my memories
of my father
in Max's Kansas City
made you cry.
   20 years ago.

Now, superimposing this lunch over a salad
of flowers,
a field of bleached poppies
in the mountains of Montenegro,
a day of names
      I remember
the rainy day Philadelphia lunch,
artichokes, their magnolia shaped leaves
being scraped in our mouths,
petals,
petals,
I remember your
dressed petals, artichoke leaves,
connecting our mouths
with Montenegrin fields.

Our incredible wish to connect!

To name
with every inscribed bite
the memories of our fathers.

from *The Rings of Saturn*

For Clint in East Lansing While I Am Sitting on the Adriatic Coast

I bought figs every day
almost.
And looking at the sea in the morning
is better than sitting in our patio
at home.
But it is the ocean I love,
not other languages or cultures.

Michigan is not the only place
where there's no appreciation for
native cuisine/ what we cannot
forget
is how civilization and imagination
allow someone to take what is available—
     the salmon,
     or the cherries,
     the asparagus,
     or millet,
     or squid,
     or milk,
     a certain kind of grape,
     rosemary growing wild,
and turn it into
a remarkable food.

And that without a real sense
of possibility,
even an imaginative dish
like pizza
can turn into tasteless cardboard
with bad tomato paste and dull cheese
as it is in dozens of restaurants

in East Lansing.

Never thought I'd get tired of
grilled meat
but after three weeks here in Yugoslavia
I did. It is variety we need some-
times. A view of the ocean
though,
perhaps if I had that daily,
I should never
want change or care so much
about the
imaginative use
of natural ingredients.

Perhaps.

from *The Rings of Saturn*

Robert Waxes the Car

Pedestrian as iceberg lettuce
a man polishing his car,
his Blue Boy truck,
his *little deuce coupe*
while I scald my morning
pot of tea.

Those falls, frothing, foaming
rushing towards crushed ice snow storm of
waters, and the doctor from New Jersey
watching the girl in the swing,
she whose skirts ruffle
like cherry blossoms.

Perhaps an American scene,
but English or French masters.
Glenn Gould plays *The Goldberg Variations*
with the precision and art of a snowflake.
Cold days cracking off
the year, and I see

the studs in the heavy cartilage of
the upper edge of Robert's
ear, no Van Gogh, but as good
as Edward Weston, refining his darkroom
techniques until each sheet of print
is a glacier of packed history.

Every day jobs he does
with the precision of an icicle hanging from
the eaves on frigid mornings.
Those too he knocks off, so they won't
fall and shatter against our precious necks.
No job too small.

Any job—to make a salad,
        to wax the car,
        remove the icicles
        hanging over our doors,
        or to print the perfect negative into flawless
        black and white,

he does fulsomely,
to present the gift of the everyday,
a kind of art,
an offering, an image,
shining,
silver,
round and perfect as the
ball studs
pierced into his upper ear.

Orchids at Oldsmobile

He looked different from the image of
a factory worker I had. Short,
for one thing, and pudgy—no muscles.
Movies have replaced action
for me, and that's good.
I think.
But what isn't good
is that they've invaded my mind
also. And now these men,
who could never star
in a film,
sit drinking like Bukowski
in the local bar.

I snap the peanuts
out of their shells with my old thumbs,
sip my chilled white wine, which I order instead of
red because cheap white wine is more
drinkable.

Remember drinking amber, that is,
Remy Martin,
when I was young
and still drank hard liquor.

They think,
"She's old, why isn't she
more interesting?" I still have not
switched into my Georgia O'Keeffe mode,
though I grow these big Moonflowers each summer,
these Datura she painted,
among other vulva'd flowers
in hopes of invoking her spirit into my life.

Bukowski knew
how to carry this stuff off,
pretending he was Hank Chinaski,
so outrageous and dynamic that you wouldn't care
how many boils he had, or how *acne vulgaris* was
        accompanied
by a nose that looked like a cartoon buzzard's beak,
and little pig eyes, and in fact
a body like a hippopotamus.

But me, I am having a hard time
carrying off this Georgia O'Keeffe stuff,
no tan any more, just age-spotted hands, arms, legs.
Even if you could see them—I always wear trousers,
long sleeves.

I kept thinking, as I looked at this Michigan
writer, that he'd
only written one book that carried off the illusion,
and asked myself if I had even written
even one
like that?

No, growing orchids,
or was it eating
orchids?

Something I wanted to do but never
succeeded at, is more or less
the story of my life in this
Oldsmobile town. And now, what can I say?

        "Why don't we look more interesting?"
                        meaning perhaps?
        "The [orchids, sic] glowed in the room,
        and she wrote by [orchid, sic] light.
        Her eyes were candles.
        Her fingers had diamonds in them
        for none to see.
        [Orchids, sic] bloom in every place like snails

144

in a rainy season.
Listen to me:
Light from [orchids, sic] is not unusual.
Turn out all false lights." ★

★ This is an emended quotation of part VIII. "Light,"
from my poem, "Fifteen Poems for a Lunar Eclipse
None of Us Saw," from *Waiting for the King of Spain*,
reprinted in *Emerald Ice.*

Having Replaced Love with Food & Drink

a poem for those who've reached 40

Sweet basil,
sturdy as my legs, aromatic from Donna's garden, its healthy
green leaves pungent
in a fist-sized bouquet on my kitchen sink.

Whirling
the leaves which I have snipped off
as carefully as buttons
in the sharp blades of La Machine,
adding both white flashes of pine nut and garlic,
a long golden drink of sweet olive oil

Al pesto
though I haven't used either mortar or pestle

My linguini simmers.

This evening alone
with my books
handsome jungle of plants,
real clay:
        Pewabic,
        Grueby,
        Owens,
        Rookwood,
on my shelves.

Yes, I have gladly given up love
for all the objects made with love:
           a poem,
           an orchid,
           this pasta, green and garlicky
           made with my own hands.

from *Cap of Darkness*, 1980

The Dark Procession Reviewed

My body glistens,
snail moon,
delicate lettuce leaf breasts,
cucumber skin,
pale moistness of early summer and
the fantasy boys I long for,
> blond surfers and skiers,
> black scorpion musicians,
> Whitmanian sculptors,
enter as solstice images:
the dream-code
marks each one.
> ("Ms. Wakoski," says my seal-sleek
> bright student, wearing corn-golden
> t-shirt and skirt over her Easter tan, the
> gold chains coiling on her neck and fingers,
> "is Galway Kinnell still alive?" She is
> preparing her oral book review. "He was
> born in 1927. That would make him
> pretty old, if he's still alive." Only ten
> years older than me, I think. "Yes, he's
> alive. He would only be about 54," I say
> firmly. Wondering if anyone
> understands that the longing of youth
> does not pass away with middle age.
> Not even with old age.)
Tonight, the full moon sits outside my window
a beach ball
and shines its light on the shadow of
my girl-body.
The moon shines on seeds of Jerusalem Cherry,
rooting into a ball of fronds for me in new soil,
and on the football shaped magnolia buds,
thrusting their scaly pistols into Georgia night,

and into my longing brain, spinning
which has been set in patterns of love,
for years,
cannot resist one more
fantasy.
I sleep long long hours
under this moon,
for the procession of lovers, always
best in imagination, is long
and while the real life is dark with pain,
with outlaws, cowboys, the military, and lovers
of men, there is another life,
of novas, young
exploding men
of light
who love me with Apollonian grace,
who worship me through poems and
letters
let the loving remain perfect
because never fulfilled.
Tonight I dream of Craig,
     who rescued my Jerusalem Cherry with mealy bugs
     from the wastebasket,
     and who haunted my office this winter, foraging
     for sugar,
     and who had just asked me to judge a poetry
     contest between him and Paul Murphy for
     the prize of pound of M & Ms,
     with his soft voice and unreadable handwriting,
     his slanting eyes and golden self in love with
     John Lennon, as
I have in the past
dreamed, luxuriously, of
     Steve, the California runner from
     my high school town,
     with football shoulders and the wonderful
     poem about eating
     Christmas dinner at McDonalds,
     who stood on my doorstep in grey
     running clothes reminding me that I dared not

touch anyone
I really loved,

or Robert, whom I longed for in Majorca,
    while he drank and ignored me,
    except for the lonely conversations we had
    in the lane by the bake shop or on the path near
    the *torrente.*
Is this the real procession
in my life?
Not dark, but hidden?
The men who allowed me
sensuousness, completely
fulfilled by the longing itself? Would
I rather fantasize
than touch?

The moon stirs this body tonight.
Pale lettuce, gone to seed,
grown tall and feathery,
a ruffled pagoda, a false shape,
the delicate leaves
we desire to make up our salad,
the moonlit lettuce patch,
pale leaves,
pale leaves, under the snail moon.
Reflected light
from the golden lover hidden behind
sea-grey eyes?

from *The Magician's Feastletters*

Opening the Sunrise

She feels it shimmering up
like Sappho through
her feet. She opens more space
into her flannel gown,
billowing out the sapphire night
and she opens
her hands to the gust/
steaming cappuccino ascending.
Now she's
wide open, a Blue Mountain gash,
a gateway of split,
morning's bean, a
portal beyond the
ocean/ she rises, rises,
above
boulder sleep
and soars, flies,
unfolds into
the perfect Adonic
of morning's *café au lait.*

IV ON THE BANKS OF L'EAU DE VIE

When Breakfast Is Brought by
the Morning Star

When breakfast is brought by the morning star,
she is imagining that she is writing in a book with white pages,
and that her coffee which comes in a thin cup will taste
like raspberries. She has been a lily all night
on a pond, and her white petals fold into a cone
as she sees the morning star who delivers the *Wall Street Journal*
folded on the tray with the china cup and the silver pot.

Water lilies, she thinks, but she
doesn't write it down. And morning glories. The book is open on
      her lap,
her thick satin nightgown is folded around her
Raspberries with cream would be nice.
Her husband is sleeping and on the pillow
his gardener's face, tanned and earthy, moves slightly with his
morning breath. He and she dream different things,
but both wake up against petals, both drink a clear glass of water,
both descend the stairs and find the morning star has brought
their steaming cups,
the fruit,
the grain.

Sometimes I miss the obvious. But often,
the water lilies break open in the sunlight, and the pond
poses for Monet. But when I stand still, I notice
all the mistakes I have made. I notice also
that I could live forever, and never live my life
differently. I still long for all the things which seemed so elusive
and which I made so many mistakes trying to find. When I wake
      up
in the morning, there is for a moment, the sense that everything
is possible. That I can rewrite my life,

that I can be a different woman. But then the morning star
serves breakfast, and one sip,
whether it be a dark fragrant tea, or a rich
oily cup of dark-beaned coffee,
one sip and I know that my life
is the same one I've always lived.
New day.

New day doesn't mean new life;
it means that you continue to work out afresh
each day
the story you were always destined
to tell.

from Medea the Sorceress

Our Lady of the Chanterelles

for Judith Minty

I love knowing that when a person opens
her hand, there is a map there,
if only you know what to look for. How to read it.

Looking into your American hand, Judith,
I see that you have surveyed San Francisco
and inscribed its arc-ing bridges
as rings on all your fingers.
You're driving your daughter the Chef over the Golden Gate
into Napa-Sonoma, on your way to white table cloths
and daily roues, drinking those nectar-y chardonnays
and wondering about how much more at home you feel
in Northern California, with baskets of Chanterelles and
        hedgehogs
rather than the wrinkled brainy morels of your own state.

In the light of Chanterelles that twist and crown you, Judith,
in Western light glinting from the sharpest knife,
in maplight, and in kitchenlight, together, you and Annie
will eat the bread of Marin County, dipped in green
olive oil and try a risotto cooked with fennel and porcini
        mushrooms,
and think of how the Redwoods
of California, and the Douglas Firs now
seem part of a Western map both you
and your daughter have on your hands.
The map of Michigan is a mitten, a throwback
to the first opposable thumbs.
No dexterous articulated fingers to accompany them.
No chef's hand so skillfully trained as Annie's; no eye
for beauty
like the one

she gets from you.
And your hands,
        Mother and daughter, traveling in mushroom light,
what do they really map or, touching,
see? A dotted road of light,
leading to the center?
Like the illumination that reminds me I am in exile?
Unable, like you, to make two maps, or is it two roads?
turn into one inexorable
set of lines
on my palm?
I could say the map
was too watery here in Michigan,
though there is no Pacific Ocean
with its primal salty broth.
My hand's map seems empty and smooth,
dry as Death Valley.

Our Lady of Chanterelles,
I turn to you. Open your hand: show me the secret,
the beauty of this aging
desolated terrain.

from *The Emerald City of Las Vegas*

Mole at Chloe's

to Wilton & Jo-Ann who prepared the feast

from Oaxaca the black tar
in a plastic tub
looks like raven Crisco, some grease
to be used for machines in the jungle but it turns
into, after many hours, a slick elegantly thin
sauce for the braised rabbit

Of course, that evening was a feast with a jar of roses
jiggling on the table just like
those Mozart roses on the European piano in a film

and the women I met, also
film women:
     Rachel who is a face and body and willful mind
     Bertolucci could love,
     quiet Martha Marie, for a Woody Allen flick,
     and equestrian mother Jennifer, of a deaf son and Dynasty
     soap opera marriage and divorce,
     all of them perhaps perfect for one of those Danielle Steele
     movies
     where women are self-made beauties who finally win
     money, fame and men.

I am there in my cap of darkness;
except when Rachel and Marie talk, it turns
to silver.
From an invisible woman
I turn into one with
a history.
My eyes are not grey
like Athena's, but because
of the black

mole
have turned silver,
slick
with anticipation,
for this meal where the food and the talk are equal.

Oh, Jo-Ann! Wilton!
Surely this is a movie,
not life?

The Tango Lesson

for Sally Potter

Lights in the cinema theater come up; only a
few of us, like the cans of hominy in a cupboard left when
everything popular has been eaten,
still sit there. We are women, except one
sleeping fat man in suspenders,
and most of us are fat too as summer ears of maize.
The bulging polyester
pants suit in the row behind me crunched popcorn and crackled
    her
bag like frying tortillas throughout
the entire film,
but it didn't matter. The music
obliterated everything, as I huddled in my own
discreet elastic waisted denim trousers and baggy jacket.
First it was *Dirty Dancing* that I went back and saw
four times, and which some woman in Detroit
said in a newspaper article
that she saw 104 times while on a reducing diet.
Why did she need to diet? When I watched it, I *was*
the doctor's slim daughter on vacation at Grossinger's
transformed into the spangled Merengue dancer, lifted in tulle
up in the air to show Daddy how good she was.

Then came *Strictly Ballroom*, more literary, more
sepia toned, yet wild with its Australian satire on
Apollonian order, the English world of regulation Ballroom
Dance, the irony of Latin Dances performed by rigid rules,
the begging for a passionate
Pasa Doble.
Once HE puts his hand on HER waist,
as tight as the silk inside a raw
earn of corn, she

moves with the natural precision of its rows
of perfect kernels. Old
and fat women, like her grandmother in this Latin family,
carry the flamenco tang into each swipe
of a broom. The competition now
is about love.
The dance scenes were
the real sex scenes. Correct that.
It was learning
to dance
that was so sexy. Maybe the reciprocity of teaching
and learning—they
are the ultimate acts of love making?

The lights simmer, modulate up in the theater. We are the
same women, I the Goddess of Corn,
too old for a life of passion
or dance.
But not for other forms of
teaching and learning.
In the movie palace, we are still all women:
Prim, prissy, scholarly and now-old tamale hips Diane.
Other women with pimpled faces
or dowdy bodies, sexless thin women in stick dresses,
parched corn women, corn husk dolls,
fat women in tents, mostly women watching
transformations.

Usually we are watching the rules
of the perfect-bodied Apollonian world
being over-turned by messy, yet more beautiful Dionysian
dancers, who dance to live,
who more precisely and beyond rules, define the
possibility of "orgy," "abandonment," "ecstasy"
as they dance, dance, dance
for joy,
for love,
making love,
yes, transcending sex.
Though in the movies, even yours Sally, they get that

160

too.

For the viewers, myself and
these other women,
it's food.
Our creamed corn eyes
melting on to the screen as we watch
the dancers.

Next there is your film, *The Tango Lesson,*
about making art, but it's the same lesson of Apollonian
rigidity and order, giving away to passion.
Only when SHE, played by you Sally Potter, dances
in the club does HE see HER
and even then he takes HER to the professional exhibition dance
stage and grinds HER with the rules
SHE cannot heartily
follow.
This film is for intellectuals,
but it's too romantic for them. Too corny.
They think it's about love,
when it's really about dance. Or they
think it's about dance,
when it's really about love.
Kind of wild.
No wonder you made an unpopular film, Sally.
No takers: a romantic film
about learning to tango
which is really about finding out how important it is
to be Jewish?

Now there is *Dance With Me* that I've
already seen twice
during this, its
opening week in my home town. I sit
through the entire credits at the end
each time
and find the
usual assortment of women,
like myself still there, waking with me

like wet cornmeal,
out of this film.

The boy from Cuba
searching for his father. This is the first of these
movies with a boy so beautiful you want
to cry. He's played by a thirty-eight-year-old actor/ that
fact makes me really cry.
Attractive actors of course in all the other films,
but in this one the boy is a young
Tyrone Power with a Cuban accent,
a Tom Cruise,
a Rock Hudson,
even a young Elvis.
And when he dances the rumba or the cha cha cha in his
black and white Zoot Suit shoes, in the
Cuban club in Houston, Texas,
you are moving in your seat with him,
cob knocking, fields full of goddess grain, corn inspired,
you are practically out in the aisle
of the theater it's so hard to sit still. You realize that you are
wasting your life, or since
you are sixty,
that you have already wasted your life.
That finally you know you should never
have allowed yourself
to find
any way to let life
interfere with dance.

You remember that your old bookkeeper mother
met your young sailor father
disastrously, of course,
        shades of Maenads, satyrs, firelight
at a dance. A public dance hall she went to on weekends,
filled with sailors, on the Long Beach pier, in Southern California,
in the late thirties. I was conceived I am sure
after they went dancing which accounts for this strange streak
of joy that runs through me, the desire to dance.

I tell myself as the lights come up
with the last moments of salsa Cubana ringing out of the stereo
that I am not pathetic like the other women there in the
theater. I am the Corn Goddess.
I may look pathetic,
but that's because I am old and not thin like a tortilla.
Of course I also have a face,
stiff as if dried with the corn starch solution
in which we used to dip our crinoline petticoats
when I was a teen-ager.
But I am not bereft of joy.
Goddess joy.
I am still the Southern California girl
who danced with excitement each summer
when she got to go to the yearly La Habra Corn Festival.

In the corridors of the mall I almost dance
out to the car to drive home and tell my husband the movie
was just as good the second time
as the first. I might even
go again tomorrow.
One more time.
Treat myself to one more
ecstatic fling,
rolled in cornmeal, flaming with chunky
salsa pumps, dancing the polenta mysteries in this
Eleusinian ballroom I always enter
through the veil
of films like
Dirty Dancing,
Strictly Ballroom,
Dance With Me, and
Sally Potter's *The Tango Lesson.*

Costa Rican Coffee

I scissor open the brown and white pack
and instantly the smell of morning
fills this kitchen. The steaming water drips through
the maker like a lover moving next
to your sleeping body in the night and putting an
arm around your torso so that you feel as if
your body is as beautiful as the Venus de Milo. How lucky
you are in this loveless world
to have a cup of coffee to start the day,
its brown tongue presses against your lips
until you feel their redness.
You aren't in a movie, you aren't
rich or happy, you aren't
even doing something meaningful with your life. It's just
a new day and you remember that
the arms which held you
during the night
have been missing for centuries.
You know
nothingness;

smell and taste its
topaz mouth.

from *Argonaut Rose*

Crème Brûlée

Her voice is like good custard, *crème brûlée* perhaps, and she uses one hand always extended as if she's balancing herself. She holds in her other hand, the salamander iron, right out of an old French kitchen that is hot and ready to scald the top of the dessert Julia brought into TV kitchens. I wanted to mention that this woman is probably not a cook, that she was a child math prodigy, that she has eyes like blue equations.

Yet how do we know what we'll be able to contribute to the world—cooks, mathematicians, breeders of whippets? Chef Child brought so much to American kitchens, but she claims that she'll be remembered for only one thing. She believes her contribution to American cooking is the small blow torch, to take the place of the old wood-fire-heated salamander in our inventory of kitchen appliances.

Last year, Judith Minty asked for a small chainsaw for Christmas. I confirmed recently that I could not be happy without bread, cheese and wine. The math prodigy asked me, opening wide her scallop eyes and speaking like *crème brûlée*, if I could tell her who The King of Spain was. "Yes," I answered, "he comes from fairy tales."

But it seemed more important today, somehow, to figure out why I thought I recognized a name like a constellation? Why it unsettled me so. When did I ever eat *crème brûlée* that was seared the way this woman's voice burned through to my past?

from *Argonaut Rose*

Roses & Grapes

on buying a dozen supermarket roses
for my mother's memorial in Southern California,
December 1998

Auntie Pearl's mulchy garden,
shaded from the California summer by Concord grapes
dusty and blue as the skin under my eyes when I have not been
    able
to sleep, the circles under the eyes
of crushed longing

This woman with dirt always under
her fingernails, and a voice
that sounded like grape seeds and broken
skins, the juice of Dionysian women who tear men
into shreds

She, whose land was sold for sub-division houses,
she, who was the sister of the junk dealer,
she, who didn't read books
but offered the grapes of summer
and grew roses when they were still

the flowers you loved almost entirely for
their fragrance,
    roses, smelling of cool cheeks that didn't
    wear rouge, fingers not pricked with sewing and mending,
    and feet as white as Sunday school gloves

She was no one
you or I cared for,
hardly remember her
as a person, but as an icon
of what we weren't.

166

The grapes pressed
between your lips to pop their skins,
the pith of pale green dew,
the clear juice,
this bunch of grapes hanging from the summer's arbor,

Grown from the dirty
fingernailed plantings
of a gardener who might have
been
the garden itself

You and I, more like the paper the London fruit seller
would wrap around a bunch of grapes,
of course to be discarded, only there
temporarily
to protect the fruit

Or perhaps like the unscented long stem
from the florist,
the rose whose starved budhead droops
limply droops
usually at once,
though sometimes not until
the second day
of waiting.

Eating Grapes with the Algebraist

for Sarah Sword,
with gestures towards Bob Dylan

o weren't they equations?/ my
blue boy, my sailor?
Who brought me those grapes
of such drowsy interior,
of greenmelon flesh?
Not you, but a spectre,
the King of Spain with gold shoes,
and how like an Empire
State Building lift
they raised my office spirits.
How I wondered,
just wondered/ o where
had they been that I had not
been able to taste them before?
Of course they weren't common,
but a hybrid Concord,
essence of an arbor.
And you playing goddess, bringing me fruit
of the past.

o where have you been
with soft bundles
of ripened September?
Where have you been
when I've been entirely grapeless?
And where, the man
I dream of, when nobody's looking?
Where, when summer's infrequent
but fractional rain
dissolves the cobwebs skimming
those inky globes?

But today, when Sarah
brought me these icons,
we sat and let in Thoreau.
Or was it a woman on her zebra,
wearing nothing but her diamonds?
Wearing nothing, drenching herself
in the hard reign
of this autumn fruit.

o grapes, where
are the fingers that picked you?
O Diane, where
are your scissors of silver
now when you need them? o where have you been,
little madeleine-bunches?
Déjà-vueing that childhood arbor?
Concords dangling out of reach?
Still, we
ate the grapes,
we ate the grapes,
we ate the grapes!
And autumn's peace was untampered.

Robert's Spaghetti Sauce

He picks the tomatoes, both
yellow and red, trembling on the
drying autumn vines so that they fall off
in his big
Hungarian hands.
The silver studs in the tough cartilage
at the top of
his ear
catch the kitchen lights. He peels the
tomatoes easily, the skins slipping off the bodies of fruit
without feigned modesty, undressing
for his erotic kitchen touch.

He himself
is warm with autumn. His solid
muscled torso as tough as tomato vines,
as fleshy as squash, as tall and heavy as a September
sun flower. He tears the fresh basil,
with its leaves like full green lips
into the pot of new tomatoes.
Several branches of the oregano he's cut when he picked
the tomatoes and basil, are stripped
into the pot.

Salt is beautiful. You see why a city was damned for it,
and wild animals let down their guard when
they have a chance to lap it up.
Robert loves salt.
And he embraces garlic, chops many
many cloves of it,
so much that when you see the hard wood
butcher block table
covered with it, you imagine
a pearl merchant

laying out his wares,
   seed pearls of garlic,
   fresh water pearls of garlic,
   a few big smooth round pearls of garlic, all laid out
by Robert, fresh and redolent for the sauce.

So this pot with the chopped tomatoes ,
olive oil, basil, garlic, oregano and salt,
augmented by a shot
of red wine goes on the simmer. I leave to
go to the twilight movie, and when I return from my
Magic Theater,
thick German, Polish woman that I am,
I don't find Steppenwolf,
I find Robert, as if he were Prince Machiavelli
ladling his sauce over the *al dente* pasta. He smells fresh
from the shower. We aren't in Italy,
just East Lansing. It is a world right out of a book
or a movie;
we don't speak. Eat
together.
Live our imagined life
in autumn's studded light.

Scalding the Pot

He smiles his jazz bar smile,
filled with double bourbons and inhaled smoke,
standing in our midwestern
morning kitchen—the
water for my tea is boiling
and I catalogue all my choices:
Assam,
first flush Darjeeling
Jasmine with star flowers
pink Rosehip, like dawn's fingers.

"I love to see you do that," he says. I'm pouring
the boiling water out of its copper vessel
into my white porcelain pot.
I slosh it around, then dump the water
into the sink. "What? Scald the pot?" I ask
smiling my library smile,
filled with illuminated manuscripts
and calf-bound volumes.

Taking care, both of us,
to think only
of the Western ceremony
of morning tea.

A Short Fable of Endurance and Pity

*for a man who finds his present
identity unendurable*

Once there was a buffalo who liked to eat mushrooms. However, he lived on the dry plains where mushrooms did not grow. At best, he could find buffalo grass, buttercups, and chicory. In fact, this buffalo had never even eaten mushrooms, but he read about them in the *Encyclopedia Britannica* and knew that they were just what he had always wanted.

One day, as he was wandering farther and farther away from his home, looking for mushrooms, he saw something in the grass which looked to him like a mushroom. But when he nudged it with his nose, it moved. Every time he touched it, it moved.

Still, it looked like nothing more than a stone, or perhaps a puffball (though the buffalo did not really know what a puffball looked like). When the buffalo tried to grab it in his teeth, it moved again. Finally, after following the round-white-thing-which-moved for almost a mile with his nose, he said, "Are you a mushroom or not?"

The round-white-thing-which-moved said, "Yes, I am a mushroom. Or at least I think I am, though I have never seen a mushroom except in the *Encyclopedia Britannica*. However, I think I look just like the picture of a puffball, and I am very happy at last to know what I am."

"I am going to eat you if you are a mushroom," said the buffalo. "Because all my life, I have wanted to eat mushrooms. I know that they are what I will like. How fortunate that at last I have found one. You are sure that you are a mushroom, aren't you?"

Now the round-white-thing-which-moved began to think it

might not be so smart to continue to call himself a mushroom, if the buffalo wanted to eat mushrooms. Therefore, he replied, "I could be a stone. Stones are inedible."

The buffalo, who was disappointed, hung his head. He almost cried, but decided that since never in his lifetime had he seen a mushroom, it was not so terrible if the present moment did not hold a mushroom. How could you miss something which you had never experienced? But there was no doubt that he was very sad indeed.

The round-white-thing-which-moved saw a tear in the buffalo's eye and that he was fighting hard to keep from crying. He himself knew disappointment, and even more truly, he knew the fascination of mushrooms, of the hours of reading the encyclopedia, of finding pictures, of learning varieties, and to him, the excitement of at last identifying himself, knowing that he belonged to a world which could describe and understand him.

And he thought to himself, "But if I am a mushroom, why am I pretending to be a stone? If I am truly a mushroom, perhaps the most exciting and real thing which could happen to me is to be eaten."

Pretending that he had not seen the buffalo's one concealed tear, the round-white-thing-which-moved said shyly, "I could be a stone, but I am really a mushroom. A puffball."

Then he stood still in the grass. Awaiting fate.

The buffalo bent his head to the ground and with his big teeth picked up the round-white-thing-which-moved, opened his mouth wide, thrust the round-white-thing-which-moved between his jaws, and began to chew. But the moment he bit down on the round-white-thing-which-moved which was now holding still, he broke several of his teeth, for the object was hard and smooth, and not soft as a mushroom should have been. He spit the round-white-thing-which-had-moved out on the ground, covered with blood, no longer looking like a puffball, in the grass.

174

To this day, the buffalo has not tasted a mushroom, for he disdains them, and has written an appendix to the encyclopedia article on how unfit for consumption the puffball is. While the round-white-thing-which-moved now moves slowly and sadly across the prairie, knowing it is not a mushroom, but not knowing what it is.

It has most recently taken to calling itself, ironically, a "rolling stone," since one day a passing car on the highway, filled with beautifully mustached young men looking over the plains, was the source of a voice calling out over the prairie, "Look. That must be a rolling stone!"

But the round-white-thing-which-moved found it hard to take such a pronouncement seriously. Nowhere in the *Encyclopedia Britannica* could it find an entry for "rolling stone".

How could that ever be his proper identity?

from *Dancing on the Grave of a Son of a Bitch*

Diet Moons

roll into her car
when she isn't looking. Like autumn
puffballs, but you can't
cook these.

No salt allowed.
Or butter.

Parkin

Simple bread for tea. Oh think of those mornings
of early rising, the coke fire to be built in the grate; think
of the skirts of soft muslin, over petticoats that drape
softly around plump bodies; oh think of the Yorkshire moors
which were so open and damp, so green and rolling,
held the spirit's desire for freedom where Wesley's religion
flourished as did the fantasies of love that girls
like the Brontës cherished. Men were the prisons, and the
         prisoners,
and men who didn't want to be
became
the worst imprisoned, Branwell
covering his pain with laudanum.

I saw those small rounded loaves, sitting
in the bakery window, just
the size of the clay circles
in which we, in Kindergarten imprinted our hands,
and sent off to be baked
in a kiln and glazed (mine was green and shiny, like a new spring
rhododendron leaf)
and I, always the scholar of new foods,
rolled their names around my tongue for an entire day:
"parkin, parkin, parkin," imagining
I would wear my black woolen cloak swirled around me
for a tramp onto the heath, and carry in a large pocket
underneath the cloak, a loaf of parkin, an apple, a bit of cheese.
I didn't know what it tasted like, until teatime, when I ate
half a mince pie, hot and sweet,
and a bit of parkin—oh gingerbread,
slightly chewy just blunted with a little molasses,
the energy of it would wave through you
as you walked in the damp cold, seeing a world
of ups and smooth downs.

I imagined one of the girls
pulling it out of the oven early in the morning,
and the smell of it
coming up through the stairway to my bedroom
where I was still snuggled and bundled into the covers of night,
with a steaming pot of tea on the table
next to the bed, the fire in the grate lit for me
by some earlier riser. So small,
these comforts:
the fire, the tea, the parkin,
then the freedom of the walk.
But everything,
when you consider the human condition; everything,
when you consider war,
or famine,
or urban poverty,
or torture.

Forget about love and its absence,
or lack of recognition for your work. Forget about
unsympathetic relatives or boring
jobs and daily life.
Remember these small things
as everything.

"Grateful," don't be grateful.
Such a chore.

Just remember
the small things: the parkin,
the fire in the grate,
the cup of tea,
the walk on the moors,
or even this human
comfort—sitting here with words,
with the yew bushes in the Michigan backyard,
covered with pillowy snow,
the bird feeder abandoned by even
our unshowy birds, but now filled,
a small thing,

waiting for the cardinals and blue jays and infinite flocks of
        sparrow
to discover we're back and offering
the small things,
cracked sunflower seeds
("50 pounds of oilers," I hear the clerk say). Everything
has its vocabulary. Another small pleasure.
Sally's voice from out of the Pacific, dripping with plum jam
"remember the small things, the cup of tea ..."

I've remembered,
thought about them as we walked in Haworth village,
ate parkin,
as we've come home to our small lives
and the small things,

"the small things," as Sally called them,
which save us from
desolation.

from *The Emerald City of Las Vegas*

Sally Plum

*for Sally Arteseros, who has
never liked her name*

velvet,
soft as a mouse,
but the color of Satsuma;
mauve silk and seed pearls;
you said you
hated your name
but don't really know of one that suits you.

Tonight I serve
Plum Pudding, soaked in cognac for a month,
its currents plump with boozy waiting.
The hard sauce is as smooth as an egg.
The bombe
in its amber pool of Remy Martin,
burning,
sustains a cloud
like blue bachelor buttons
or swamp gas,
will-o'-the-wisp caught on a plate.
I think of autumn bonfires
in a world of pumpkins, wheat and sheep.
The reddleman camping
in his van,
a lonely figure walking over a moor,
on a crackling night.

In a drawing room somewhere
with another name,
perhaps Elizabeth or Charlotte or Mirabelle,
you would be wearing your new plum coloured velvet
with a bonnet to match,

and then you would dream of another time
when there would be more to do than
reading
or singing Schumann.
And you would wish your name less staid,
more friendly,
a name like Sally
which might allow you to travel unchaperoned with a man
in a railway carriage; or
would you long
for another culture?

black hair?

rice-white face?

in a land where the blossoms of cherry
or plum might offer the life
of a Geisha?

a name like Satsuma/
               Sally Plum?

Some say we are
what we eat.

from The Magician's Feastletters

Eating a Plum on the Terrace

This plum is something I never tasted when I was pregnant
with no husband.
It tastes the way my hands feel when
I hold them against my lover's tentacled muscles
at night, the curves that yield with sea urchin sweetness.
This still taut plum
is the color of raw squid skin, and its interior
tightly soft
like a jelly fish. It was lying unchilled
this morning
on its Chinese dragon platter
in a fragrance that might draw bees,

I walked past it and smelled
summer, I bent my head
over it and four other plums, inhaling
the odor I would think
love ought
to smell like. Not that seawater brine
smell that is sex.
                  We ought always
to be lying in beds with fresh linen
smelling of lavender, and then the darker coral fan
of this fragrance of plums would
come out of our bodies
as we touched.
Even the excretions should smell
like purple ripe plums,
though they don't.

Eating it this morning
was like making love
the way love
ought to be made,

by young or old, by singles or
couples. The plum had been lying there
ripening from its rocky supermarket beginnings
for almost two weeks. Just yesterday
its fragrance almost made me
pluck it; but I waited
until this morning,
for the sunlight
on the porch, the gold
that preserves
morning, allows it every day
once again to be pure.
First I showered
and made myself clean, the silver-gold
of my hair
also shining, and I walked
downstairs,
picked up the plum from its Chinese platter
took it out on the terrace
and ate it finally, slow bite by slow sweating bite,

holding a white, perfect white
napkin under my chin,
my hands like sea anemones breathing in and out,
savoring the way in which the present can be
better than the past,
middle age more fulfilling
than youth, love in the sunlight
more complete than sex
in the moist dark.

After Edward Hopper's Marbletop Table: A Sestina for Anne Waldman

I was surprised to see you, Anne Waldman,
your hair once again ash blond and a bit Veronica Lake-ish,
since you looked too glamorous
for the Suburban you were driving down my main street
that always looks like an Edward Hopper
painting at night.

But I recognized your sun glasses, opaque as night-
club doorways. It was one of those cataloguable Anne Waldman
sun-slanted mornings, the depression diner images of Edward
    Hopper
cafes flooded over, washed now as golden as Veronica Lake
looked to Alan Ladd when they drove through their noir-ish
    streets.
Still in the sky, last night's full moon was quite glamorous,

No, unbelievably glamorous
because its translucent tissue paper image transcended night
and bobbed up high over East Lansing's daylit main street.
I was wishing we were both in Manhattan, Anne Waldman.
I was glad I was not living in the age of Veronica Lake,
the Black Dahlia, or the forties, as portrayed by Edward Hopper.

I had just bought my cup of Irish Cream coffee, not at an Edward
    Hopper
diner, but at the Fragel Bagel. I was also glad I wasn't in glamorous
Paris, drowning in a Veronica Lake
of words, themselves wearing the dark glasses of Paris night.
New York, Anne Waldman,
has always been my city. Sometimes I wish I still lived on East 5th
    St.

184

with the Motorcycle Betrayer. His street.
Instead, I sit here bent at my Edward Hopper
Marble Tabletop, and you Anne Waldman,
passing through Michigan to more glamorous
places are bored after only one day, one night,
sneaking out past the poetry guards, a trench-coated Veronica
    Lake,

yet not really like Veronica Lake
who disappeared behind her blond hair. I know my main street
well after twenty years of Midwestern living. At night
it will always be like a painting by Edward Hopper,
and remind me, as do you, that even a moment's flash of
    retrospective glamour
is what poetry's all about. Yes, Anne,

Anne Waldman, who appeared with your risen moon Veronica
    Lake-ish
glamorous blond silhouette, even tho it was morning on my main
    street,
today you too lit my Edward-Hopper-diner-painted Midwestern
    night.

The Dangerous Hermit

for The Motorcycle Betrayer

She's not crazy, just doesn't like
to explain herself. She eats pecans
fresh little ears in their paper boat shells
and thinks of how
those shells are as smooth as
a certain hand.
A flash of her Wanda Landowska arms
poised over
the harpsichord, the green silk
of the moon, the terror
of virtue—these things make her into
a hermit. She doesn't want
to have anything to do
with people.

Or animals. She doesn't
like them any better.
What happened?
What lover refused to touch her
and spread green silk
one last time,
or disappointed her
when she offered him pralines out of her smooth
hands? She
wasn't a Southerner, so no
excuses. She's just a woman
who doesn't accept lies.

She's really not crazy, though she
probably is dangerous.
After all, she believes the zebra is always there,
waiting for her, at least if she's naked.

And even though she doesn't like animals.

She rides away from everyone,
naked, and obviously wearing diamonds.
But if that's her disguise, why couldn't he see
the Wanda Landowska arms,
the crescent of moon under her foot?
Perhaps he'd not notice the pecan tight nut of her
hidden sex, but the smooth pecan skin
of her bridling hands? Surely he would see that?

When the moon unrolled, under
zebra-light hooves, its immense bolt of
green silk, and she rode past him, he should have

oh, he should have—so many things he should have.

We think we see everything,
but of course
we don't. It's the moon. Always
the moon. Spilling its
splashy silk, its nightly ocean.
Who is listening?

Finally we find out:
that's why she's
dangerous.

Light Poem for the Lion Painter Who Bakes Scones in Michigan

for Hank DeLeo
with thanks to Jackson Mac Low

And with all of us sitting at a table thinking
how nice it is to sit in the afternoon's
tea light,
especially when it means eating the scones
which Hank baked, and which gave out such beautiful
scone light,
it was entirely beyond even
the light of crumpet, muffin, bagel, or croissant—
it was simply, exotically,
scone light.

Hank DeLeo
in scone light.
Baking scones in the farm kitchen
in scone light.
Making paintings of feathers which look like flowers
sometimes,
in scone light.
Loving his beautiful wife and building her a room
full of bookshelves so that she can work
in palladium light,
but she goes for inspiration to the kitchen
where Hank is baking
in scone light,
with the cat curled up on the couch, also
in scone light.

Diamonds of sweet-textured dough
that we hold in our hands.

So beautiful, I let him know.

He paints them with egg, he lets me know.

Steel Man eats three.
With jam.

Dainty Alice eats two.
With honey.

Moon Diane eats one.
Plain. She is
savouring every morsel. Before
the afternoon is over, she will
permit herself others.
With jam. With butter. With lavender honey.

Jackson Mac Low: "Good artists are good cooks."
We owe him for *The Light Poems*.

And Hank for giving us a *Light Poem* day.

Sestina to the Common Glass of Beer:
I Do Not Drink Beer

What calendar do you consult for an explosion of the sun?
And how does it affect our poor histories?
The Event might be no different to our distant perspective
than a whole hillside of daffodils,
flashing
their own trumpet faces; or a cup of coffee, a glass of beer.

A familiar thing to common people: a beer,
when it is hot, and the sun
flashing
into your eyes. Makes you forget history's
only meaningful in retrospect. While flowers, like daffodils,
only have their meaning in the fleshy present. Perspective

cannot explain sexual feelings though. Perspective-
ly, viewing a glass of beer,
we compare the color to daffodils
and perhaps a simple morning view of the sun.
The appetite is history's
fact. Common. Dull. Repetitious. Not flashing.

Suddenly, without explanation. The routine of bowels and lips.
    Flashing
past like a train, they come. No previews or perspective.
Sexual feelings are unexplained, as unexpected beauty. History's
no good at telling us about love either. Over beer
in a cafe, you might stay up till sun-
rise, but even that's routine for some, as every spring returning
    daffodils,

waxy, yellow as caged canaries, spring daffodils
make me want to touch. Is this the flashing

disappearing feeling of love and sex the sun
also brings to my body? With no object, no other body's
        perspective,
only the satisfaction of self-wanting completion? I wdn't order
        beer.
I'd order a cognac or wine instead. History's

full of exceptions, and I think I'm one. Yet, what history's
really about is how common, recurring, we all are. The daffodils
once planted, really do come back each spring. And drinking beer
is a habit most ordinary men have. The flashing
gold liquid recurs in war, in factories and farms. The sun
has explosions that we do not know, record, or ever keep in
        perspective.

Thus, the sun embodies more of the unknown than most human
        histories.
We get little perspective outside ourselves. Ignorant of daffodils
flashing at me each spring, others sit *al fresco* drinking beer

from *Waiting for the King of Spain*

V GREED, PART 14: THE GREED FOR PURITY

Green Snake, when I hung you round my neck
and stroked your cold, pulsing throat
        as you hissed at me, glinting
arrowy gold scales, and I felt
        the weight of you on my shoulders,
and the whispering silver of your dryness
        sounded close at my ears

Green Snake—I swore to my companions that certainly
        you were harmless! But truly
I had no certainty,

        from "To The Snake," Denise Levertov

    This is where the serpent lives, the bodiless.
    His head is air. Beneath his tip at night
    Eyes open and fix on us in every sky.

    The stars are putting on their glittering belts.
    They throw around their shoulders cloaks that flash
    Like a great shadow's last embellishments.

        from "The Auroras of Autumn," Wallace Stevens

1 Now the serpent was more subtil that any beast of the field which the lord
   God had made and he said unto the woman, Yea, hath God said, Ye shall
   not eat of every tree in the garden?
2 And the woman said unto the serpent, We may eat of the fruit of the trees
   of the garden.
3 But of the fruit of the tree which is in the midst of the garden, God has
   said, Ye shall not eat of it, neither shall ye touch it, lest ye die.
4 And the serpent said unto the woman, Ye shall not surely die:
5 For God doth know that in the day ye eat thereof, then your eyes shall be
   opened, and ye shall be as gods, knowing good and evil.

        from Genesis, Chapter 3, The King James version of the Bible

    And they are three, the Gorgons, each with wings
    and snaky hair, most horrible of mortals,
    whom no man shall behold and draw again
    the breath of life

        from *Mythology*, Edith Hamilton describing the
        Medusa and translating from Apollodorus

PREFACE TO GREED, PART 14

The Night Rides of My Neighbor, Lorca, That Prevent Sleep

Outside my window
coffeecups have scented the breath
that blows my curtains,
        sleeping,
                leaving stained rings
                on that counter,
                my face.
Dreams move my countenance
as if it were earth
being pelted by rain.
With any horse he rides,
my dream must try
to move as fast
and here I am
painfully awake
remembering
that I have been put in charge
of all the gold
in this world.
        Only I
can keep it polished
to its right
color.
Dregs of coffee threaten
to poison my life,
to stiffen my fingers.
           Why
have I been put in charge
of all

this beautiful soft metal,
this gold?
Will I have to spend my days polishing,
or if not that, inspecting,
looking at cups,
handling rings,
waking up to find bracelets waiting at the foot
of my bed?

Have I
the strength to keep travelling,
have I the loud harsh voice to keep urging and scolding
those slaves, the mere owners of
all objects made of this soft metal?
It rustles in my sleep
like curtains. It clinks
like coffee spoons. It invades my knees,
ankles and wrists, threatening to stiffen me to the
breaking point; I dream
at night that the gold covers my eyes wetly
and seals them shut. Am I
the only one who can tell
when gold objects are polished to the right luster?
Am I the only one, Lorca,
that you can trust,
riding through the night, invisible, as you do,
knowing this world has forgotten blood on the lips
of your flowers.

My own
soft lips bleed endlessly, darkening with clots
from all my angers, and yet my blood
is so thin, they will not transfuse it to strangers;
I hear you
riding by, ready to stop again this night,
torturing my dreams in restless steps I cannot
keep up with; you are coming to increase
my assignment,
to tell me I must be in charge of all the silver too,
for under my care the gold

of this world begins to
shine and remind us
of the desert and its simple ordering.
>Another dream comes to torture me.
>This time about rattlesnakes frozen and placed
>near the head of the bed; as I grow warm with sleep
>the snakes begin to thaw, their unstable blood to flow,
>and they will crawl down over my face.
>Fighting with more hands than I should have,
>I try to hold them off.
Lorca,
why are you riding around so fiercely,
frightening me
that the gold of this world
will lose its luster and disappear
without my constant
articulate
care?

>(c. 1971)
>from *Smudging*

NOTE

I have prefaced this new part of *Greed* with a poem I wrote in the early seventies. I remember writing this poem when I was at Yaddo, the one time I ever went to one of those artist's colonies. I spent my whole time there hating the mediocre (as I judged them) writers and musicians and others who were guests along with me. I even left early, and I canceled an invitation I had accepted for the MacDowell Colony later in the year. Said I'd never go to an artist's colony again, as they catered to would-be artists. I haven't, though now I think my judgments were too harsh.

I assume everyone reads in that poem my obsession with poetry or my versions of Apollonian beauty i.e. gold. In retrospect, this poem reminds me that even before I had culminated my on-the-road poetry life and entered academia (Writer in Residence at Michigan State University since 1975), I was already fiercely fighting—perhaps windmills, but what I thought of as the battle for true poetry, pure poetry, the best poetry, the gold, or whatever you want to call it. How could I have been so sure that I knew what it was? In one sense I am not, or I would not anguish so. Yet, in some way, I have never questioned my own fidelity.

For years, I have tried to strike a balance between accepting the general ignorance of poetry most people—even educated people—have, along with my own strong opinions about what's good and mostly what's not, and my dedication to teaching and preaching poetry in the purest way to serious students. But the anger builds, even though I constantly search for ways that I can demonstrate my opinions objectively. I diligently try to steer students away from fraud and stupidity in both the writing of poetry and the world of publishing it.

I suppose there is raging in me a classic battle between the extremes of Apollonian and Dionysian behavior. While I am perceived by the world as a Dionysian (Diane-isian?) woman "dancing on the grave of a son of a bitch," my desire for Apollonian beauty and order are what govern my poetry and the way I view the poetry of others. I pour out my feelings, my instincts, then actively search for ways that I can defend what I believe to be good, with rational analysis.

Unfortunately the Dionysians see me as up-tight; the Apollonians as out of control. I know that I have earned a reputation among other poets for being a mean or bitter person because not only can I not gratuitously praise any poetry, and most especially that of trendy or prize-winning poets, but also I feel compelled to publicly denounce or condemn such poets or poetry. This "honesty" has made me a tormented woman. My obsession about purity is obviously eating me up. And thus I am ready to try to find a passionate and cleansing way to voice this. To exorcise this greedy obsession. I hope this is what I offer in "Greed Part 14."

One final note: I hope that the careful reader will enjoy in this poem the allusions to alchemy and the hermetic mysteries that have long intrigued me. The multiple quests for purity, gold, a balance of sun and moon, male and female, and the tempering of self that has been in my life and poems for nearly forty years come together in "Greed, Part 14." Or, so is my aspiration.

THE GREED FOR PURITY

Coffee on the wind.
Light comes in,
and out goes the night motorcycle
rider. Black leather jacket. I
put on my boots
and he steals
my scarf of gold.

PART I

Gloves of Fire

Alchemy

Strindberg nearly burned
his hands off, in his attic room
in Paris, trying to turn lead
into gold, not understanding that money
didn't prevent him from writing. All
the young men I know
think money
will solve their
problems. I know that money makes
things better as long as you don't have to think
about money or how to get it. But once those subjects
become gloves of fire that you wear, burning
your hands into the shape of ragged paws,
you might as well be poor as rich.

. · .

I live in a state where people see The Northern Lights,
though I have never seen the Aurora Borealis.
I read and read, looking for
a new way to understand that tempting fire serpent
guarding the Golden Fleece but
I am his sister. I too guard every hint of gold and silver,
and have no respect for history unless
it echoes my vision. For instance, I
cannot fall in love with the later poems of Wallace Stevens the
    way
I love his early gift. Stevens that master!
Yet I refuse to grant him greatness for his later poems.
Diane, the Keeper.
Stevens alludes to the serpent in the sky but

now that we know that there are auroras over the poles of
Saturn, now that we know that having a
"mind of winter" isn't as breath-taking as
he found it, now that
we know that we can cut DNA chains up into
scraps, why is it that
I, at least, still don't know what single serpent
Stevens saw? It was those lilting waves
of Northern Light, serpenting through the sky,
but many of them, colored as neon,
not a single tempting snake,
a singular voice
such as the one I see and hear.

Perhaps he was thinking of the Delphic oracle,
The Pythoness who hissed her prophecies
in sines and sinews of smoke
out of the most beautiful earth I have ever seen,
the hills of Delphi?
I, the Freudian, would have seen sex in the sky, yet
Stevens doesn't seem to care
much about that subject. So what is
that multi-lighted serpent to him?
The garden of Eden?
Not phallic,
but colonic?
The serpent of fecal decay?
Were you meditating on waste, on shit,
on death that is not breathless and icy and pure, Mr. Stevens?
Were you meditating
on swamps and sewers, which may be
biological images of life
but which, to those of us who are living,
seem like the image of decay and repellent death?

I wish Clayton Eshleman could still be friends with me,
oh how I wish that,
even though I have never really understood
his scatological vision. Perhaps
Eshleman dismissed me from his table

because I could not understand Stevens' serpent
in the sky? Or simply because I have never read him,
Eshleman,
with the reverence I accord
that earlier poet? And of course, everyone knows I only read
the early Wallace Stevens. Certainly
I have not thought that the reason I was banned from Clayton's table
was that I had no idea that Stevens too
had found a version of "Hades In Manganese,"
that I was rejected, as I have rejected so many others,
my gold seen
as dross.

My own sky is blue today, the color I associate
with a summer dress, with a girl in a swing, with another
girl with blond braids and fire bees buzzing around the yellow
      ribbons
in her hair. I see no serpent there.
Inside my old body, little ripples
of blue pleasure
respond to the idea of auroras
over the poles of Saturn though,
as if there is silk clothing for this old woman,
as if there is rose and blush and a perfumed bedroom
with a lover waiting. The ice, of which Saturn's rings might be
composed, is clear
pure, not touched
by animal cycles
that produce waste
and are the scene of
regenerative life.

How does anyone
put these opposites together? Or if she does, how can
she stand to wait for the rest of the world
to catch up, to see the Saturnalia
an oxymoron of auroras,
to find beauty and teach those
spoilers
not to touch it?

Refrain

Coffee on the wind.
Light comes in,
and out goes the night motorcycle
rider. Black leather jacket. I
put on my boots
and he steals
my scarf of gold.

PART II

The Midas Chocolate

If she doesn't eat her chocolate
and the other children do
she'll still possess those rich bars, dark
as coffee beans,
when no one else does.
The sweets go stale as dead campfires in her pockets, the
other children don't play with her, she
has only
her pride. Holding out.
Not eating the chocolate
when the other kids in loose J.C. Penney's and Sears Roebuck
    clothes
ran on the playground, played tether ball,
went skating after school, stopped
together at the candy store on the way home,
ate their candy, while she kept hers
in a pocket and stayed
pure.
She had something they didn't.
She gave up pleasure
to have something everyone else
consumed; she held the taste of it outside her body,
never physically savoring it, and she told them,
and then they ran out to play,
not inviting her along.

In her pockets, the oily candy melted
into its wrappers, then hardened again. It bloomed to
grey, tarnished silver, the oxidation of chocolate,
now not beautiful except
in her mind. It was there, her chocolate,

transformed to metal, her Midas sweet
that made her rich,
if not golden, at least
veiled silver, from her un-consuming
touch.

  . . .

She wore her blouses, her coats, her
clothing, high to her neck, always the top button
buttoned. They teased her, even her boyfriend
teased her, "Diane, unbutton the top button of your coat;
it's 80 degrees today." She held out,
as she held her candy when every other kid
ate theirs. She stayed buttoned up.
She wore nylon stockings to school.
She held herself aloof. She
held on to herself, and everything she
could have spent or the way
she spent it. No comic books or movie magazines,
like her sister. Nothing she
wouldn't want to save.
At once she learned that saving something
meant giving it up. That is, if you saved your chocolate,
you couldn't eat it. If you saved your allowance
you gave up instant gratification, a term
she learned as she was reading psychology, especially
Freud, but many others too.
She confused pleasure and sacrifice.
She felt she had so little,
and was so greedy, longed for so much more.
She was a stale chocolate,
  or should we say a "saved" chocolate,
in a pocket,
held away from everyone.
Pure. Midas pure.

She had one on-going nightmare.
Often she dreamed that a tall, broad silhouetted man
like a raven with his wings widespread
cut through the screen of her always open

206

bedroom window in her
small town Southern California stucco house.
Started climbing into her room, wearing his black turtleneck
    sweater
and Navy watchcap, his black gloves and black trousers.
She would wake up, her throat straining to
scream, and the darkness
would seem thick with
the intruder. She would be
too frightened to climb out of bed
to close the window
—the diamondback rattlers might be on the floor and strike her
    feet
She never stopped being afraid of the dark.
She held herself close.
Saved herself, wreathed in fear.

Playing the piano was where she saved nothing.
Where she spent every
silver coin.

Refrain

Coffee on the wind.
Light comes in,
and out goes the night motorcycle
rider. Black leather jacket. I
put on my boots
and he steals
my scarf of gold.

PART III

Finger Ears

By then she was addicted
to touching the keyboard, alone in a room,
the sexual touch of Beethoven or Chopin was complete.
But to what purpose?
Where could she live, practicing the piano five hours a day,
knowing she didn't sound that good
to the world? How live as someone whose passion
was only a hobby in the eyes of the world?
So she gave it up.
Cold turkey, as addicts often do. Decided to spend her time
doing something for which
she had always received praise, something which
was easy in an unlimited way,
for her.

The purity of holding the chocolate in her pocket, not
eating it. The purity of no longer
touching the keyboard,
not ever, not even to play a Christmas carol
at a party, or occasionally while an evening away
with her old scores.
To hold herself away.
Never touching.
Not ever touching.
That was important.

Now she listened. Now she listened with every
part of her body, as if everywhere there were fingers reaching
out of her ears, touching the keyboards that other
pianists played. She heard, she touched
everything

as piano music. Every word
was a touch from her reaching fingers.
She found a way to keep her purity,

touching

words into scarves of gold.
Polishing the metal in her pocket
into silver rings, bracelets,
chalices.
Touching everything
now with the ear-fingers, aloof, held away from
tactile ignition.

Beware anyone
who threatened to violate this
purity.

.   .   .

Now there was darkness
only lit by gold,
the gold that burned, glowed, in her un-touching Midas fingers.
Beware anyone who tried to touch that gold.
Beware anyone who offered gold
and shone only gilt.
She was the judge. She
was The Keeper.

.   .   .

Gold In Her Mouth?
    Crowns.

Silver in Her Mouth?
    Fillings.

Who was the betrayer, the thief?
    He was someone who left after touching.

Who was the lover?
    He was someone else.

210

Did you make love with a pilferer of gold, a thief of silver?
Yes, but he was someone
else.

Was he golden, a
hero?
Yes, he was a Jason wearing the golden fleece
around his naked shoulders.

Why did you help him steal it?
It was mine. All the gold was mine.

Was he a silver arrow?
Yes, it is still lodged inside my pocket with the chocolate.
With my ears, I finger its metal
every day.

Refrain

Coffee on the wind.
Light comes in,
and out goes the night motorcycle
rider. Black leather jacket. I
put on my boots
and he steals
my scarf of gold.

PART IV

Medea's Summer Eyes

And the enchantresses of
a certain race
had eyes that appeared golden. As
if the sunlight radiated out of them, and even
penetrated the dark
of a cave.

But Medea kept her eyes
lowered, a modest woman,
so in love,
the arrow adding to the film of bewitchment
cast over her eyes, so that Jason
who appeared naked,
pure, and an object of longing
to any maiden,
could not see her goddess gold.

Did he, even for a moment,
forget his target,
the golden fleece, as he shot his bow
against her body? Did he ever
look into those eyes when he made love to her? Did he
ever see their light? Perhaps he thought
enchantment ruled her in a different
way, that her eyes recorded
the golden fleece itself?
Were a sign that it was his
for the taking? So
he took her,
she willingly; he
a warrior.

Can there be any other history
for warriors? Taking and using any weapon
provided by destiny,
or is it chance?

Robert's Yellow Tomatoes

The goldfinches of our summer garden:
these low-acid, sweet, yellow skinned tomatoes.
I've picked a bowl of them.
Just the ones as gold as Medea's eyes,
gleaming their sulfur/chrome enchantment to
the gaze of all of us
who love the taste of tomatoes.
Warm
from the summer garden,
our means for recognizing
the taste of The New World
where this "poison fruit," nightshade beauty,
tempts
everyone.

Soon some of them will be a shimmering topaz platter
of translucent sliced flesh, ornamented with slips of emerald
fresh basil. It's the basil I taste first,
then the salt I've added, then
follows the taste of
tomato.
What is that taste, I
ask myself?

It is the gold of Medea's gaze.
It is the prize Jason lied for
in his seeking. It is the purity
of youth.
Or love. Are they a concord?
It's the taste I'd have
if I could be young again,
if the boy from my youth could be
kissing me again,
the taste of excitement that emerges every summer
when the goldfinches return
to our backyard feeder.

Refrain

Coffee on the wind.
Light comes in,
and out goes the night motorcycle
rider. Black leather jacket. I
put on my boots
and he steals
my scarf of gold.

PART V

Goddess Gold

I need to hear
your stories.

First we are served with spaghetti in bowls,
al dente like crystallized ginger,
and it's covered with a fresh tomato and basil sauce
that has the kind of sweetness I associate with a boy holding
a kitten under his sweater in winter. Frangible
beauty extends to foods
when you think of them with each bite.

The red wine makes me think I am
outdoors in Italy, a family table
eating this pasta *I Primi.*

I Secondi comes on hot ceramic plates,
lamb chunks stewed with Green Sleeves green beans
from John's garden. "Leg?" I ask.
"Shoulder," says Jim. "Oh what a task to butcher," I groan,
and he says the butcher at Goodrich's did it for him.

I smile and say that I find it hard to delegate
any labor.

There is a gusty quality to the meal that the hearty red merlot
supports. I continue to feel as if I am in the good part of a movie
like *Stealing Beauty*, Bertolucci's film which takes place
in Tuscany during the summer. So far, the food is more interesting
to me than the people, though they are all friends with whom I
    feel at ease
and often they are the people who stimulate my imagination almost

as much as a book or a film. But tonight I am
tired and just enjoying the table,
the foods of summer. I know a ripe Howell Melon
comes at the end, another golden object,
a princess's ball to play with.
We grow up and eat it, consume the gold, now
that we've lost our purity. But what about truth
and the way it keeps contradicting our pleasures?

How did I suddenly find
myself saying all the usual things I ordinarily say with
my friends, trying to keep the space around me intact, often
        fending
off others' opinions that
would infringe? How do I find myself
suddenly being yelled at,
breaking the quiet murmur of the well-fed room,
riveting everyone's eyes on me as my friend angrily shouts,
"you never listen, Diane"?

To what don't I listen, I think, not even quite aware of why
he's yelling at me, perhaps proving that I haven't
been listening
as I have no idea what could have made
this usually so mellow man
so furious.
Instantly, I shut down. Now I really am not
listening. I am trying to keep myself from crying.
I am trying to encapsulate myself. Trying to hold the chocolate
in my pocket, feel pure and aloof.
Feel as if I have kept,

held,

preserved

what others consumed. The
precious metal in my pocket, in my accusing eyes,
in my confusion.

I think I understand somewhat
why Ezra Pound became silent in his last decade.
Didn't speak. He had spent his life speaking, and gotten locked up
    in
St. Elizabeth's for it. I think I appreciate
religious men and women who take a vow of silence,
thinking perhaps I might do that myself. After all, it's not that I
    haven't listened
that has aroused my friend to anger with me,
but what I have said. Surely he knows that? Surely he isn't
    complaining
that I don't listen, but that I say something different
from what he thinks?
I have spoken something that pushed him
into furious shouting. Yet, during the conversation I was fending
    off
    —with smiles and shrugs and occasional mild retorts—
both him and my friend John,
    who grew such wonderful green beans,
both of whom were spouting ideas I found difficult
and to me, derogatory,
if I chose to interpret them that way.
I hadn't.
For it was just dinner conversation, and I was more interested
in the food
than the people.
I didn't want to quarrel, only to make
a space
around myself,
one that no one could invade,
violate, or attack. I needed to keep myself pure,
to cherish the gold, the silver perceived with my Medea eyes.
I failed.
Silence
would have been the most successful gesture I
could have chosen.

How I admire you, Ezra Pound, walking Italian streets
where Charlie Baxter saw you. Black clad,
but perhaps of the race of sorceresses? Perhaps with

golden eyes?
I don't know how to deprive myself of the spoken word,
though I have such an affinity for silence.

The day after being denounced
by my old friend I started
on a reducing diet, one that forbids pasta, beautiful melons,
and wine. I have stayed home alone for weeks,
feel peaceful.
But I can't get out of my mind
hearing my friend of twenty plus years
yelling at me, the worst thing he can think of to say to a friend.
"Diane, you don't listen."
We haven't seen each other since.

He is married to a goddess, a golden woman.
Why does he have so little patience with me, his old friend
just trying to live her Georgia O'Keeffe life
in the desert of East Lansing? Well, go ahead and accuse me of
self-pity. All my life I've complained about injustice, unfairness
and most people have called it
self-pity. Yet silence is not a good opponent
for injustice and unfair treatment. It participates
in a way I still can't allow myself.

"Silence is golden"
admonishes one of our great maxims.
I can hear Jason jibbing me,
his irony dripping like hot solder.
How can I, the silver sorceress, ask myself not
to speak out?

Refrain

Coffee on the wind.
Light comes in,
and out goes the night motorcycle
rider. Black leather jacket. I
put on my boots
and he steals
my scarf of gold.

PART VI

Raven or Serpent

He opens the car door
and we walk to the picnic table.
Gold coins float through the
air, fall around
us. No one picks them up.
The trees do not save
their leaves.

.   .   .

There are candles on my shopping list.
For over a week now, looking for the blood stain,
then forgetting to buy the candles, then dreaming of the man
with big hands

the Motorcycle Betrayer, whom I haven't seen for twenty-five
        years.
I am thinking of him
because I seem to have to explain myself to
everyone these days. And I don't seem
to be very successful doing so.

"You don't listen!"
Clint yelled furiously at me during a dinner party,
but how can I with my
finger-ears
that reach out to touch every word
in a Midas gesture
laying what I hear into the gold scarves of poetry, I
with my finger-ears of
un-consuming touch, I, who have
replaced the sensuous touch

of the keyboard
with my
un-touching finger-ears, I,
the one who listens even in the night, be told
"Diane, you don't listen!"

I had insomnia for hours, then when I
fell asleep I dreamed of the Motorcycle Betrayer, a
     shape-shifting dream where
     he turned
     into someone else.

     The black raven man. But now he too assumes
     another form. I thought the snakes were fire,
     dragons, guarding
     the golden fleece, but now there is one whose
     pterodactyl form, long serpentine neck
     is onyx, obsidian. Is he outside my window?
     Cutting the screen?
     Coming in through my childhood
     window? Am I still enough,
     hidden well enough in the bed,
     that he will not find me?
     My dream shifts to the black motorcyclist,
     his helmet like an ebony moon outside our window
     as I wake up ululating
     an eerie wail.
     Robert is frightened awake and I say, "I'm sorry, I'm
     sorry, I was having a bad dream."

How could anyone listen as well as
Clint's wife Judith, who listens like a sponge with a 180 IQ. You
     feel she
drains you of your idea, and absorbs it, makes sense of it.
It is orgasmic listening.
And Clint has been spoiled, living with her.
But Clint is partially right, I don't listen:

Not the way Judith does.

I hate so much of what I hear. I hear so much that
simply is wrong, then I try to argue with it,
try to make my finger-ears
transform it into my own gold,
which later on the illuminated page will be tested
beyond the coffee scented breath
of a thief. But when I argue,
the gloves of fire leave everything ragged and charred.
There is no gold, only my black raven fear
and my anger at the violation.

I think that's Judith's strength. She probably hears more that is
     wrong
than I do, but she doesn't argue with it. She
just keeps listening.
I listen for a while until my finger ears feel ravaged
and burned. Then I give up, and then
Clint is right: I don't listen
any more.
I hide my gold, I hide my silver,
I hide it all,
against the Raven
always waiting to cut through the screen,
to throw the black cloak of winged night over my charge,
dulling it
to absence.

Refrain

Coffee on the wind.
Light comes in,
and out goes the night motorcycle
rider. Black leather jacket. I
put on my boots
and he steals
my scarf of gold.

PART VII

Nighthawk

How I love the opening of
morning. But I need sometimes
to see how closed each daily session is
with more than night's knotted shadows, yes,
so that I can watch
it open, the vapor rising
not just
from the ground
but from sleep and closeness.

Morning sunshine
    lifting into a
        scarf of gold.

   .   .   .

This is the purity I seek and which causes me to be as abrasive
as pumice. Trying to file down the rough intrusions
against order, symmetry. I tell a student,
with passion, that she is "what is wrong with the whole art world,
especially the world of poetry," because she is asking
for school funds to start a magazine of her own,
without even having investigated working
on the official campus student magazine.
"Why not?" I ask
    "I didn't know there was a literary magazine on campus."
Ignorance.
Ego.
Yuppie Gold Medal Mentality?

She wants to be the
editor, the star. She wants to be important.

226

She wants to have her name on the top of
everything. She is a beginner. She is talented, rather smart, but
knows nothing about poetry. She doesn't care about
poetry, or art, she cares about being
important. Having an official title
to put on her application to grad school, her
resume, her letter to her successful lawyer of a father.
I tell her that she needs to learn her craft before she takes charge
        of art.
I tell her she needs to work her way up an hierarchy before
she takes charge. I tell her about the purity of
art, how it is beyond ego, beyond success, or fame.
How the value of writing poetry is the quest for complexity,
purity, truth, all those things which are elusive
and never paid for. Beyond price, a cliche,
but the only thing I can offer her.
I have given her the purest metals in my chest.
Polished, luminous.
She wants glitter, but not this.
She hates me, an old woman. She wants
to rip off, shred the
scarf of gold.

She threatens to sue me, the department, and the university
on her father's letterhead,
a missive to the English Department written in the form of a legal
        brief.
Everyone
is upset, especially me. She asks that I
be publicly dishonored
and fired for "abusing" a student. She craftily bargains
to be dropped from my class and given an instructor who
        guarantees her
an "A" for the term. She keeps us all in thrall,
though I suppose I should thank her for the hours
of thought and writing I put in,
trying to understand whether I did something wrong,
trying to teach purity,
whether I was misunderstood or actually wrong,
trying to believe that there was something meaningful

in the time I spent
examining my role as a poet
trying to pass on
the Olympic flame of our tradition
to a young aspirant.

The matter continues to haunt me, though in practical terms
it disappears. All she wanted was
her "A" in poetry writing and no one
to challenge her power. After that year, I decided
that there was no longer
an "ivory tower" to hold those of us who live for purity,
at least not in the form of a public university. I felt glad I was
     older
and within a decade of retiring.
I lost my previous assumption that people really want
to be exposed to The Best, the Most Worthy or Excellent.
That is why they attended university.
I had to face what so many of my friends faced
years ago, that perhaps
all students ever wanted
was to be praised.
Whenever I could not do that gratuitously,
I would always be *persona non grata*.

Nothing new. Diane holding the Midas
chocolate in a secret place,
keeping herself pure. Aloof.
Again, the price of not being silent.
Ezra Pound, that year I walked invisible with you
around the city wearing black trousers, black jackets,
a priest's black brimmed hat.
The gold I was polishing was not real gold. I rubbed off
its gilt; she published her magazine, disappeared
from my life. Neither I, nor my other students ever saw
this magazine however. All that fuss
for something no one ever saw!
Another university funded "accomplishment" for her to put on
     her
vita, her résumé, her application for grad school,

228

meaningful to no one, though listed as history.
Self written history.
The coffee wind is always bitter when
it intrudes through the dream window.

Refrain

Coffee on the wind.
Light comes in,
and out goes the night motorcycle
rider. Black leather jacket. I
put on my boots
and he steals
my scarf of gold.

PART VIII

Polishing Light

Saving is renouncing.
Holding back is giving up.
The little girl with her chocolate uneaten,
nestled into her pocket, saved
so that she could have something other children
did not have.

Trying to keep herself pure
Not buying other kid things like
comic books. Not unbuttoning her top
button, practicing the piano as if she were eccentric Glenn Gould,
but not ever being that genius. Then giving it up, after
fifteen years. Having a baby, her boyfriend's baby
when she was eighteen, and giving it up.
     He didn't love her she found out; she couldn't marry a man,
     create a family with someone
     who didn't love her.
     Surely the most impure thing—such marriages.

She would save herself like chocolate,
not sexually, but emotionally,
for the man who would love her
as she loved him. But she, like the oxidized silver chocolate
bloomed into the Ice Queen, or Medea with the downcast eyes.
Or to many, The Medusa, snakes of icy anger
and fiery snow radiating from her head.
She was in an ice cave, dark as Arctic Winter.
But beautiful to herself,
perhaps only to herself,
with the gold she cared for,
polished,

like *Das Rheingold*, guarded by the Rhinedaughters in wavy
    depths,
the gold for which she had sacrificed being ordinary.
Yet, she always felt the sting of loss
when her handy work was praised in others, ignored in her.
She saw fool's gold in every public place, mica more
adulated than her own metal. Always in disguise, a witch,
enchantress, magic,
never perceived as a goddess.

.   .   .

The woman from Santa Fe tells me that she remembers an old
and valued friend,
now dead,
talking to a now-famous poetry
critic, in an elevator in New York City.
In the sixties. The upshot
of the story:
they both,
even my friend, now dead,
dismissed my work while praising the woman from Santa Fe
as the real thing. Pure gold.

Unlikely, I think,
but even if it's true, why is she,
my friend from Santa Fe,
telling me this?
    Wanting me to panic again
    with dreams of the black nighthawk
    cutting through the childhood window?
    Coming to steal my gold?
    Or worse, to cover it with the wing of metal bloom?
    Taking away its shine?
    Leaving the woman from Santa Fe there
    as the only gold?

    Yes, she is telling me
    that she is
    the only gold. Yes, I recognize
    the ugly echo of self when I see it

232

reflected in others?

Then I realize we're all polishing gold. The famous
critic, my dead friend, me, the woman from Santa Fe. Each
trying to dismiss the other's gold as illusion.

    .   .   .

Referring to me, another critic says, "despite
her disregard for craft …"
even though I am one of the most finicky
craftswomen around.
"Someone to watch," he says as if I am thirty, not sixty.
"A good book," he tells libraries,
"but only for big collections."
No more reviews for that book.

    .   .   .

Robed in Tyrian purple, Maximus of Gloucester, in "Letter 5"
scourging Vincent Ferrini and all
editors of little magazines who publish each other,
quid pro quo, rather than searching for gold. He rages,
but he too appoints himself
—as do I and so many others—
the true crucible in which
gold can be proved. How to avoid
the fatuous indignity of presumption with these tasks?
How not to cheat ourselves,
outwit our passions? The absurdity
of polishing
light.

Refrain

Coffee on the wind.
Light comes in,
and out goes the night motorcycle
rider. Black leather jacket. I
put on my boots
and he steals
my scarf of gold.

PART IX

Meeting the Ice Queen

Is it presumption or courage that has made me
spend so much time
quarreling with masters as well as idiots? Or only the sliver
of the Ice Queen's ice in my eye?
This Master
once invited me to dinner in her down town loft
when I was newly arrived in New York City, 1960. But it was
     purely a
gesture, dictated by someone else, and she had no sense
of the Midas chocolate burning in my pocket
or by now
the sliver of ice lodged squarely in my eye.
I quarreled with her, left in a huff; she was, I now realize, another
version of myself. Also
     obsessed with purity.
     Also
     totally righteous in her views.
The gat-toothed enchantress,
 dancing with a green snake around her neck,
"re-learning the alphabet" and often "wanting
the moon".
She angered me then, and often later
with her own presumption, as she continued to
thrill me with her incantations.

"How can you admire her, be enchanted by her?"
asks the woman in Santa Fe
     whose voice has replaced her body
     whose ragged map of her life has been thrown out
     so that now, on moonskin, she's redrawing it.

235

"Because, though she didn't know it, she
passed her job on to me,
the job of polishing all the gold
in the world until it remains
only a blur of lustre.

Don't you understand?"

No, she doesn't.
Though she'd never admit it. I am like her too,
rewriting the world to shimmer the way
I believe it should, chiding everyone who does not
have the same vision
of beauty. Of perfection.
I ask her what "moonskin" is,
but she can't hear me.
I'm too far away in a land of white summers
and I am never sure where
my task is taking me.

Oh Diane, Diane, who hates all poets who are
awarded MacArthur "genius" grants.
Who longs for the Pulitzer Prize but has something
uncomplimentary to say about every poetry book that wins it.
Diane who tells her good friend her poems do not contain
completed tropes, and expects her not to be insulted,
who rants about a perfectly good writer, a beautiful young
woman poet whose mother
is a famous sculptor
saying that she is an "airhead," another example
of the childhood allegory of "The Emperor's New Clothes,"
in fact beguiling intellectuals
into thinking this is poetry because the discourse
is so abstract and her appearance so
seductive. Who wonders why people might see her as bitter?
Diane, Diane,
who rants against poets who are
politically correct
and hates those who, in her view, pose
as victims, usually interchangeable with the politically correct
        writers

or those who excuse their bourgeois lives by "witnessing,"
Diane, Diane, who thinks that if you are rich
you probably can't
write good poetry, and discounts one of America's
favorite elite poets
because he was the heir to millions.
Diane, Diane, who wonders why people
think she is mean?
Diane, Diane, who has a million prejudices—for instance,
how could someone who is so involved with being a mother
possibly be a good poet?—who
judges people personally but abhors them
for so-judging her,
how can she delude herself that this is
idealism?

Diane, Diane, what snake is in your garden,
whispering to you
that some forbidden golden apple, or
silver apple out of Yeats' garden of sun and moon,
could be yours? How could you
expect ever to eat this apple of the knowledge of truth and purity
and not be thrown forever
out of the garden of poetry?

Refrain

Coffee on the wind.
Light comes in,
and out goes the night motorcycle
rider. Black leather jacket. I
put on my boots
and he steals
my scarf of gold.

PART X

Desert Carp

You're in New York alone, walking
as fast as you can from Houston Street where
you've seen two films at the Angelika film forum, eaten
a scone and drunk tea, and now
are trying to make the five o'clock showing of a film at the Quad
on 13th Street in the Village.

In the twilit slant of sun, your cap of old hair looks
golden—like an ornamental carp
swimming in a pond.

You know that you could live your whole life like this,
going to the movies all day, beginning at 11 a.m.,
walking from Manhattan theater to Manhattan theater,
watching three, perhaps four, movies in a day,
looking only at strangers, finding
intimacy through a camera lens, and if
you were rich/
no, if you lost all your ambition,
much of which is fading as you age,
then you might move to New York and do nothing
but go to the movies.

Of course, you'd run out of movies.

Then someone would say, "why don't you write about movies,
      Diane?"
And I would say, "Who would listen to me if I said
Pauline Kael is wrong about so much?
If I said that Hollywood's greatest movies are teenage stories
and romantic comedies?

If I said people don't understand purity; they understand
pretensions to art ?"
So maybe you are better off, as the carp?
Your hair glinting in the sunlight,
your old hair.
Reading as you do, seeing lots of movies as you do.
But one thing is definite:
You should not talk to anyone.
Fish are silent.
For all practical purposes anyway.

I see the carp in this pond
some almost orange, some golden, some faded to
a tuna white. This is the day when
someone looks at my cloche of swimming gold hair
and then opens a book
that I have written. It's not in my head, it's
on a page and my hair, like gilt deckle
on the tips of the pages, reminds them that they have no
right to try to change my vision.
I am the carp,
swimming in my own golden patterns
that glint to silver
tarnish.

Let them watch. Let them watch.

In my dreams, as I once said, I am a rational man.
Yet they yell at me, they argue with me, they steal my
expanding rooms of silver and gold,
or they just ignore me.
I carp. Is all of life a pun?

I carp. Golden. My hair glinting
like Medea's summer eyes.

. . .

Holding oneself close,
the feeling that all has been stolen,
stripped from one.

Empty now, or incomplete;
or that The Complete is not possible;
this is not what you started to do; this is not
what you sacrificed for,
is it Diane?
This emptiness is not purity,
surely not?
It is time to relinquish the task.

It is time to savor the moment,
trying neither to preserve nor keep it. And certainly no longer
to change it. The moment
is all there ever was.

It is a moment
when only you can see rooms full of gold:
The world's gold,
polished to its full luster.

By the morning sun.

Cherish the fact that you might be the only
one who sees this;

then despise not the others who
claim their gold;

despise not the others who
do not see yours;

do not try to pass on the flame to anyone
who doesn't come asking for its fire;

be silent
and let yourself own the morning's splash;

turn your eyes away from night
and others' prizes.

The Raven man coming in the window

—remember!
he never actually comes in, only
coils out there in the
desert night to
frighten you. Might his black moon
too be inverted light?

Another secret of beauty?

Diane on your morning terrace,
the blue dye of silk
against your plump white arms;
Diane with bare feet,
rose-colored with fear that you'll
lose your morning's purity.
How can that happen?

Only you know that this gold exists.
It is not the destruction cutting through night's
window that you have
so long feared. It is a voice,
and not a voice,
murmuring over the submerged
siren-fingered Rhine Gold.

Refrain

Coffee on the wind.
Light comes in,
and out goes the night motorcycle
rider. Black leather jacket. I
put on my boots
and he steals
my scarf of gold.

PART XI

Honoring the Discovery of Zero

When I sit at this table,
reading the woman who walked with an enchanted green snake
curled around her neck, so many seasons
beyond her critics, beyond even
me, one of her best readers,
I who
thought she was
a sorceress,
know why she was most of her life "wanting
the moon," the silver one she saw reflected in the water.
But I could not
tell this to anyone important
in my life.
I have not been able, even, to
write this in my letters
and so much, thus, has gone unsaid.

I know when I look into my bowl of tea
what everyone sees
who looks down a well:

> Wanting something we can see, even though
> it's not there, that zero reflected in the well
> from the Moon in the sky?

> Trying to polish gold that is only
> morning light?

> The danger
> of believing it's all in your head,
> not that *that*

isn't true,

just that it's dangerous
to think so.

What is missing then
is like zero,
a quantity, though it seems not to be. I've said before,
zero is love, oeuf, egg,
procreation. We're all in that trap,
aren't we?
If I can have each morning complete,
why should I need
any more?

. . .

Appearances

"I noticed that you were very concerned
with appearances," she said.
Why not?
Every story is about
the connection between appearances
and truth.

My dried roses
in their golden bowl,
like women who whisper to me
all day.

. . .

In the dark,
there are no appearances. How can there be
truth?
My world gradually shrinks
in the dark to one dimension. I am flat,
and everything around me only
a facade.
I feel so enclosed,
worse than going into the MRI vault

over the head and body.
Night traps me
into its flat angles
reminds me of the body's prison,
the lie of death, with no truth,
no release.

    .   .   .

But morning liberates me into the whisper of veracity.

Refrain

Coffee on the wind.
Light comes in,
and out goes the night motorcycle
rider. Black leather jacket. I
put on my boots
and he steals
my scarf of gold.

PART XII

Morning's Scarf of Gold

Silence & boiling water
mean that
it is my own kind
of morning, when the day is
complete as a pearl,

No one presides,
the palm is open. The pearl lies on the
pink flesh and is
the past
dry, closed, brittle as seed.
Easy to scatter.
Pearls before—dot, dot, dot.

Done. Now we have
the day ahead, the boiling water
poured over tea leaves,
themselves the husk of some other past,
but now eroding their amber
into my cup,
the stain of pleasure slowly
changing the boiling
water into a libation. This is purity.
This is the gold of poetry and art: this silence that is so
eloquent it is both a toast
and a prayer.
The day is mine.
I hold its purity to myself.

      .   .   .

This morning looks different, though

it's just an hour earlier
than I usually arise. The steaming cup is
the same, the precious quiet
the same. And now

I can imagine, with the sense that the
morning's condensation
is rising only
an inch off
the groundcover, that the night creatures
are still on their way home
to burrows and trees and caves. Now,

I can imagine you came
to me in sleep
across a clot of deceptions
so thick it seemed like
night. Now,

I can translate you,
the one who is there but is not. Lying next to me
the not-you is wandering somewhere
else, but I saw the veritable you sitting
at our dining room table
with your work glasses on a rope,
your chin silvery with a day's beard stubble,
your big photographer's hands,
Hungarian hands, at rest
as you told our friend the story

of identity's deceptions. Of your encounter in deserted Nevada
with an old sheep dog on the dusty road—only
us travelers and a thousand sheep. Different visions:
the driver and I, afraid of the clench of mountain sheepdog jaws;
you simply playing in the road with an old friendly dog.

I know you are a different man sometimes,
am struck with this
when I look out and see the ground haze lifting
at this earlier hour in autumn.

A man I've never met except in sleep,
our bodies so close, our minds
so separate.

Refrain

Coffee on the wind.
Light comes in,
and out goes the night motorcycle
rider. Black leather jacket. I
put on my boots
and he steals
my scarf of gold.

PART XIII

The Morning of the Enchantress

I too am a different self.
Slats of Light
against our wisteria
fence, shimmer like water,
and bolts of morning
light pour like silk into partially filled
bottles of opened wine
now labeled to
ferment
into vinegar,
pricks of each ray dazzle
drops of condensation inside the
flasks, and

autumn angles force
every vine
into grape clusters as purple as
night's wing. Now,

it is the morning of the enchantress.
I can see the green snake curling around her always young neck,
turning to radiance as the sun
burns through my vinegar bottles..
Am I seeing how gold is perhaps only an image
caused by light? Now,
can I accept how needless it is for me to polish it? Now,

need I fear either the theft of gold or its neglect? Now,
finally, do I not feel something ornate?
    Something beyond metal or liquid, or even the sun?
    Something, perhaps, like awe?

252

Should I not rejoice?
  This gold will never lose its lustre, despite purloin or misuse.
  And fiery snakes of it will always radiate from my old
  Medusa head.
  Smoky fingers of it curl out of my ears. Look.
There she is. This is no deception. The fearless dead
  enchantress!

  Beyond such petty thoughts,

  dancing in Raven light, zero light.
  Though she could not swear it was harmless, I
  now know. Seeing

  her coiling green snake—oh yes! become a scarf of gold.
  Transformed,
  falling,
  burning,
  around her neck.

Refrain

Coffee on the wind.
Light comes in,
and out goes the night motorcycle
rider. Black leather jacket. I
put on my boots
and he steals
my scarf of gold.

From Previous Collections

PREVIOUSLY UNCOLLECTED

Printed November 2000 in Santa Barbara &
Ann Arbor for the Black Sparrow Press by
Mackintosh Typography & Edwards Brothers Inc.
Text set in Bembo by Words Worth.
Design by Barbara Martin.
This first edition is published in paper wrappers;
there are 250 hardcover trade copies;
100 hardcover copies have been numbered & signed
by the poet; & 26 lettered copies with an
original holograph poem have been handbound
in boards by Earle Gray & are signed by the poet.

PHOTO: Robert Turney

DIANE WAKOSKI was born in Whittier, California in 1937 and educated at U.C. Berkeley. She has published twenty full-length collections of poems and many other slim volumes. Her most recent collections from Black Sparrow are *Emerald Ice: Selected Poems 1962–1987* (1988) which won the Poetry Society of America's William Carlos Williams Award in 1988, the four published volumes of *The Archaeology of Movies and Books* and *The Butcher's Apron: New & Selected Poems including "Greed, Part 14."* She is currently Writer in Residence at Michigan State University.